Dear
Future Husband,

Cally Logan

B BRIDGE
L LOGOS

Newberry, FL 32669

Bridge-Logos

Newberry, FL 32669

Dear Future Husband:
A Love Letter Journey While Waiting for God's Best
by Cally Logan

Printed in the United States of America

Library of Congress Catalog Card Number: 2022947299

International Standard Book Number: 978-1-61036-160-6

Edited by Lynn Copeland

Cover and page layout by Ashley Morgan

Interior design by Genesis Group

To the Lord Jesus Christ,
to whom I owe everything

Hello

Dear Reader,

Letters. Even the mere word drifts our thoughts to yester-year when soldiers would romance their sweethearts an ocean away, or lovers would flood pages longing for a day when the space between them was replaced with the embrace of being together. Letters in themselves encapsulate a nostalgia within our hearts that we may have never experienced. Handwritten letters bring to the modern age a rare gem of expression, offering a great ability to grow the anticipation and feeling of love.

For the past twelve years I have been writing letters to my future husband. Though I began writing without even knowing him, they hold within them the promise that indeed one day I will be standing by his side for the rest of my days. My hope is as that, you journey through the pages of this book, you will find yourself within these letters and perhaps feel inspired to capture parts of your own life as a "message in a bottle" that will one day be given to your earthly dearest.

If nothing else, I pray these letters will inspire you to pray for the man God has just for you. He is real, he exists, and he is walking on this earth right now. God knows both of your hearts, for He created them both. So, as we journey forward into these letters, consider this man of mystery and remember that his heart is waiting to meet you too.

All my love,
Cally

First Impressions

April 23, 2011

Dear Future Husband...Whoever You Are,

H i. I'm not so good with introductions, but I figure by the time you read this we will be very much acquainted. So, perhaps I can move past the awkward pleasantries and speak as I would if we were friends. More than friends...best friends, kindred spirits, soul mates.

I am writing to you today because there is something within me that feels as if I know you already. Not in the way that I know your phone number, or even your first name, but somehow this letter will be received by someone my soul could, in a way, already recognize or know. In the same way that Adam knew who Eve was the moment he laid eyes on her in Eden. There is an inner feeling that as I write these words they will be received, not only some day in the future, but even now as I pray over you. I believe that, through all the galaxies and mysteries of the universe, you are out there—my one and only is out there—and that God Himself would help you feel my prayer and words for you this very day.

Life seems to be changing so rapidly, and with it great milestones are occurring, and in truth I am sad to have you miss them. And so, I had the hopeful aspiration that perhaps if I recorded the changes of life and the ponderings of my heart as they occurred, you wouldn't feel as if you missed a single thing. That perhaps my scribbles and thoughts and journey would instead help you feel as if you were there too... and perhaps along the way you could come to know me as I become the woman who will one day marry you.

I recognize in my own naivety that I am but an eighteen-year-old high school senior, and I will be the first to admit I am not ready for marriage in this very moment, but one day I will be. Just as much as this is a note to you, my future husband, this is a note to my future self. For she is the version of me that you will fall in love with, make memories with, and say, "I do" to, but she would not be the woman she is if she was not first me. A young gal with bright eyes and a hope for all that is to come.

And so, welcome to the year 2011. Life is a divine mystery and, if I am being honest, it is hard to place a safe bet on what might happen next. I have sent off my college applications (finally) and await the final answer from universities within the next few weeks. Curious if you will be there at the college I choose... A fanciful daydream wisps through my head that there we will both be, moving into the dorms. It will be my first year, and perhaps your final year. I'm carrying my crate of old vinyl records that I cannot part with when our eyes instantly lock, no words will be found to escape our mouths, but all is said with that gaze of meeting a friendly stranger whom I will one day call "home." Or perhaps you are not there; only time will tell. Until then I will continue to create wondrous scenarios in which we meet, but somehow in my heart I know God will author one better than even my vivid imagination can muster.

Homework awaits and Dad and I are watching the Packers game later today. Wait, are you a Packers fan? Ah, so many curiosities I have about you.

All my love,
Your Future Wife

Prayer:

Father God,
I pray today for the man You have chosen to become my husband one day. I do not know him, but You do. You know him infinitely more than I could ever imagine, and You are building him up to become the man he will need to be not only for me, but for Your kingdom as well. Father, please be with him today and please give him a hope within that there is a girl out there very much excited to one day meet him. To marry him, to do life with him, and to be his one and only.

In Jesus' name,
Amen

A Milestone to Share

June 25, 2011

Dear Future Husband,

My graduation from high school was pretty much as you would figure. The typical speeches you might expect were given, one of them by yours truly as president of the honor society. We had a celebration party complete with a Costco cake and a few copies of *Oh, the Places You'll Go!*, but really what floods my mind are the inescapable thoughts of what awaits me on the other side of summer.

I have sent in my acceptance for Randolph-Macon College, and although it is not my first choice, I am confident and perhaps even a little suspicious that the Lord has His reasons for sending me to that specific school. It is wild to think that after all these years of tirelessly studying and preparing for this very time, I am here. Papers are turned in, tassels are turned, and all that I must do now is step forward into this great unknown. I grab my metaphorical knapsack, fill it with all the dreams, wishes, and hopes a girl can muster, take a deep anticipating breath, and step into the next leg of this journey called life.

Part of me wonders if I am really doing the next right thing. Is college really the next right thing for me, or is it just what society has conditioned us to believe the next right thing is? I find these questions ping-ponging around in my own head, but there does not seem to be a clear answer. At least for now. And so, for the time being, college would appear to be the next right thing. Did you have any of these questions after high school? Goodness, I am so curious to know more about you. Where you are from, what you hope to do in life, what your story is…

In the course of things, I am finding myself with some growing pains at home. There is a strange feeling now of having the freedom of an adult yet feeling like a child within too. I can vote, I can buy lotto tickets, I have a job and a car (even if it is a bit of a clunker), yet I feel like only yesterday I wasn't allowed to cross the street without my mom's permission. There are some tensions at home too that I am legally an adult, but I am still under my father's roof, so as you can see there are some obstacles there. "Growing pains" is an accurate term for it, remembering the excitement that I might grow a little taller, yet experiencing the aches of what that actually felt like to have my legs lengthen. Like the excitement of receiving a paycheck but the aches of actually having to show up for the job. You take the good with the bad, I suppose.

My head is swirling with *what ifs* and all of the present. Hopefully things will get a little simpler once school starts, but it's hard to say. So, for now, thank you for humoring my many curiosities and compiled thoughts.

All my love,
Your Future Wife

Prayer:

Father God,
The future is a mystery, and the present is, well, also a mystery of sorts. I pray for the today and I pray for the tomorrow for both my husband and I. Please give us the wisdom we need for this day and the wisdom we will need today in order to walk into tomorrow well equipped. Please give us level heads and hopeful hearts. All in all, help us to live lives that would make You proud.

In Jesus' name,
Amen

A New Chapter Begins

October 7, 2011

Dear Future Husband,

College is a lot harder than I thought it would be. I've been in school for about six weeks now, and to say it's been a whiplash of culture change would be putting it lightly. There are so many new things—some good, some bad—and so many questions boggling my brain.

One question that keeps emerging is one of the oldest of all time: Who am I? Not just, who am I? but, what am I really on this earth to do? For the past twelve years I've worked hard in school to prove myself ready and good enough for college, but now that I am here, I am unsure what I really am supposed to do. There also remains a tug of war between what I was taught at home with my family, my church, and my friends, and what my professors and peers are encouraging me to believe. We are not just talking about belief in God or not (that is not something I am battling) but ideas like, is it all planned out ahead of me, or do I make my own destiny? Does it matter to

God what choices I make? Should I be asking Him for input? In the answering of these questions, something tells me I am en route to finding out more about the complexities of life and more about who God is and who He made me to be.

There also remains the fact that I am not a partier. Not even a little bit. These kids can go hard—not that I went to a party, but I saw one dude passed out in a flowerbed yesterday. There are some things in this life I am perfectly fine not jumping headfirst into. Like flowerbeds.

Friendships are coming along, thankfully. There are some kind gals that I met the other day in class. We bonded over the mention of a closing sale at a store in the mall, and it turns out we have a lot more in common than the love of bargain hunting. We are even considering meeting up for lunch once a week. There is a peace about them that strikes me that they might be fellow believers too, which is something I need right now. It is hard to be in the throes of such a new place and new culture, and my heart is aching for some sisters right about now.

Classes are decent overall. No surprise I am doing poorly in my math classes, but to my surprise psychology classes are going very well. I might just explore a little more deeply that entire field; who knows what might happen. It is evident that in the course of things I am learning what it means to stand on my own feet. To grow and learn and open my mind and heart to how the world is far bigger than this campus or what is in the present. Onward I go, ready to find what awaits me down this road. You can rest assured it will be shared in these letters.

All my love,
Your Future Wife

Prayer:

Dear God,
There is so much I long to know, so many things I question within my own little heart. Lord, please reveal more of Yourself to me, and please reveal more of Yourself to my guy. Help us both come to a place where we can stand firmly without doubt when others seek to oppose us, and help us to have an open mind and heart to things that You wish for us to know more of. Prepare us for what You have for us, and please answer the questions that arise along the way. I want us to know You more, Lord.

In Jesus' name,
Amen

Dodged a Bullet

March 15, 2012

Dear Future Husband,

Well, I just got back from a date and it certainly with no doubt was *not* with you. My goodness, it was just plain awful.

I met this fellow on campus and at first impression everything seemed to be charming, even out of a movie, I dare say. You know the scene, boy meets girl. The tale as old as time where he notices her across the lawn, walks up to introduce himself, and her cheeks darken with a crimson hue as he makes her feel that she's the only one he sees in the crowd. They exchange numbers and plan to grab a bite to eat, maybe take a stroll under the stars. Magic, right? Well, I sure got that one wrong.

When I arrived for the date it was very clear that he had no interest in really getting to know me or respect me. My grandmother used to say, "A girl must kiss a lot of frogs before she finally finds her prince," and although that sentiment applies here, how sincerely grateful I am that he did not receive a kiss from me. We met up at the restaurant he had selected, but then he changed his mind about going inside to eat and suggested we just grab ice cream instead. That was completely fine, and I had no problem changing plans, though I wish I had eaten something before I went. What struck me during the evening was that the once charming man was more interested in trying to convince me to go back to his dorm with him instead of listening to a single thing I had to say. This mystery man also fully revealed he had the mouth of a vulgar sailor and a lack of really any respect. I caught him gawking at a few other ladies as they came into the ice cream parlor as well. I promptly left without even a polite, "See you later." In the words of Cher from *Clueless,* "As if!"

As disappointed as I am by how tonight went, in many ways it only gives me great hope for the days to come. Perhaps the consolation prize of it all is that I know tonight was not the final destination; it was a mere pit stop on the journey to finding...you.

I cannot say what our first date will look like, or how we will meet, but I am coming ever more into a peace that it will be a story that God alone can write. Knowing me, I will still be that blushing awkward girl who debates for thirty minutes what shade of lipstick to wear, can barely take a bite of food from nervousness, and rambles on for far too long about a random book, but maybe, just maybe you'll find that captivating in some way. What I can promise is that I will be authentically myself with you. I will not hide the things that weave together to make me, me. I will talk about the Lord as if He is my best friend, because He actually is my best friend. I will ask you about details big and small because I really love getting to know the whole of a person and not just the Cliff Notes. I will remember every single one of those details and hold them close to my heart because if they matter to you, they'll matter to me. And lastly, I will pray for you every single day, today included. I can't pick up my phone and call you in this moment, but I can lift you up in prayer. And so tonight I will do just that, as I will every night until we both reach those Pearly Gates of Heaven.

All my love,
Your Future Wife

Prayer:

Father God,
Tonight, I lift up my future husband. Lord, I am thankful for tonight because this was a night that I was reminded not to settle for what is easily available, but rather to value myself as You value me and to wait for Your best. And so, I pray for the man whom You have deemed Your best. Please surround Him with Your peace, love, and assurances tonight. Guide him as he grows and learns and becomes the man You destined him to be, and Lord, please bless our future together. I pray even from this very night that it would be You weaving together the tapestry that is our story, and that hopefully not too long from now I will be sitting at a table with him sharing the first of many meals we will have together. Lord, let him be close. Please.

In Jesus' name,
Amen

Pursuit

February 22, 2013

Dear Future Husband,

The idea of pursuit has been greatly on my heart these past few months. What is it that exists within us that enacts the drive, the ambition, or the push to pursue something or someone?

For example, take these letters. There is within my own little heart a passion that exists causing me to scribble down these thoughts, hopes, and ideas to you. Within them is the sentiment and woven prayer that indeed you are coming, that indeed you are out there, but the view outside the window of the coffee shop where I am writing this does not include you yet. Yet, I write on.

There are so many more places where we will feel the invitation to pursue, to carry on, and to embark onward. Whether it is toward God, toward each other, or toward goals or dreams, each of them requires something beyond our current views to stand in faith and belief that there is more.

Ephesians 3:16–21 is one of my favorite verses:

I pray that out of his glorious riches he may strengthen
you with power through his Spirit in your inner being, so
that Christ may dwell in your hearts through faith. And I
pray that you, being rooted and established in love, may
have power, together with all the Lord's holy people, to
grasp how wide and long and high and deep is the love of
Christ, and to know this love that surpasses knowledge—
that you may be filled to the measure of all the fullness
of God.

Now to him who is able to do immeasurably more
than all we ask or imagine, according to his power that
is at work within us, to him be glory in the church and
in Christ Jesus throughout all generations, for ever and
ever! Amen.

What this verse means to me is that, because we are rooted
and established in love, we then can grasp what is beyond our
little lives. We have access through God to believe for more,
to step toward more, and to audaciously hope. Through the
leading of Christ and the direction of the Holy Spirit, we
can pursue more based on what He has planted within our
own hearts.

Now, this has the caveat that such seeds of hope must be
planted by God and within His will, but what follows is the
journey toward the harvest of life.

Looking outside this coffee shop, it is the dead of winter.
The trees are bare, their branches laden only with dead leaves
that refused to fall. It looks hopeless, pitiful, and barren. Yet not
one of us stands in fear that the fulfillment of spring will not
come. Though it tarries, the hope of spring is right around the
corner. The hope of new life, of bursts of blossoms cheerfully

reminding us that the same God who plants the seeds of desire within our heart births spring before our very eyes.

So, I continue to write and pray and dream and hope for you. My deeply rooted prayer established in hope, my long-awaited spring.

All my love,
Your Future Wife

Prayer:

Father God,

I pray for my future husband that Christ may dwell in his heart through faith. And I pray that this man, being rooted and established in love, may have power, together with all the Lord's holy people, to grasp how wide and long and high and deep is the love of Christ, and to know this love that surpasses knowledge—that he may be filled to the measure of all the fullness of God.

Now to Him who is able to do immeasurably more than all we ask or imagine, according to His power that is at work within us, to Him be glory in the church and in Christ Jesus throughout all generations, for ever and ever! Amen.

Lord, bless this mighty and noble man whom You are growing. May we not give up on the arrival of the spring to come.

In Jesus' name,
Amen

Downcast Thoughts

December 13, 2014

Dear Future Husband,

I know it has been quite a long while since I have written, and for that I do earnestly apologize. As much as I have been trying to keep my usual giddy optimism alive, more often than not there is a plunging defeat of my emotions and hopes. As much as there are attempts to encourage myself, stay hopeful, and not fall prey to depression, it is evident that it is there.

King David has become quite the kindred spirit these days as I read the psalms. Psalm 13:1,2 states,

How long, LORD? Will you forget me forever?
How long will you hide your face from me?
How long must I wrestle with my thoughts
and day after day have sorrow in my heart?

Perhaps these days my feelings seem a bit overdramatic, but for this moment they are very much real to me. I ache and I hurt over being alone. It is Christmas time and every single one of my friends is in a relationship. It seems that any time I even get interested in a guy there is a sinking feeling in my gut saying, "No, he isn't the one God promised." When I do take it to the Lord in prayer, He reiterates that sentiment, and though I ought to be thankful for His protection in withholding you, there is an ache about the empty seat at the table, if you will. It is there waiting for you; no one has taken your place.

It is a feeling of being overlooked by God. With all these friends in these serious relationships, no doubt "ring by spring" will prove a very realistic fate. Am I wrong for being so happy and joyous for them, but at the same time longing to have my turn? Longing to have a happily ever after for myself? David's words resonate with me: how long will I be forgotten? How long must I wrestle with these thoughts and the sorrow that is so atrociously loud in my heart? Yet as these thoughts come over me like a heavy wet coat, there is no room to air them or express them to others. For in doing so I fear that their own joy will be taken, or my words will become misconstrued and seen as a jealousy. It is not jealousy that is the issue, for I do not long to have their boyfriend or their relationship. Truthfully, I sincerely long for my own name to be called. I long to be desired and wanted, and I long for the day when God finally offers, "Yes, it is time."

The Christmas season can prove a bitter chill in the air because of what is missing. The lack of a warm hug to come alongside on these freezing nights, or the mere fact there is nothing to cause a blushing hue to overtake my cheeks. Instead, they remain icy pale. In a season that is so often captured in card and photograph as a nostalgic memory, all I have the desire to do is to retreat within myself, to become detached from it all in order to somehow preserve my own heart from further decline.

Even as my pen hits the paper, I recognize how unhealthy these words sound, but there also exists the fact that it is better these words are released than for them to fester within and cause the condition of my spirit to become bitter.

Do you feel the same? Are there times you too find yourself crying yourself to sleep at just wanting to find someone at last? As much as it would be helpful to have a finger of blame to point, there is not one. There is the very real possibility that it is you who needs the work, but it is equally possible that it is me needing some sort of refinement and change. Or perhaps it is just that we have not yet reached that part of the story of our lives. I suppose you cannot jump chapters of the story that are vital to the development of the characters, but that answer does very little to soothe and balm my aching heart.

So here I am, in vulnerable honesty of where I am today. By the time this is read I will be far from this feeling, but remember today after reading this to love on me a little extra. For within the girl you hold in your arms there exists the girl writing this letter, the girl who feels forgotten and dampened in spirit. The girl who is sincerely trying to be obedient to God but feels alone in the wait.

All my love,
Your Future Wife

Prayer:

Father God,
Please remember Your daughter. Please remember me in my ache and hurt, and, Lord, if Your son, my future husband, is feeling the same, please provide him with the comforting peace that only You can give. Please turn Your face upon us both this day, for it is You and You alone who can grant us goodness at long last.

In Jesus' name,
Amen

More Thoughts Per My Last Note

January 4, 2015

Dear Future Husband,

After re-reading my last letter to you, I realized there are some places in my own heart and head that really need some checking. It is not wrong or sinful to feel depressed or downcast, but there are places that really do need some help. That help cannot come from within me; it must come from the outside, but it can be received by me graciously.

That being said, I have decided to lay before the throne of God my desires. I want to take time off from even the idea of dating and really make Him the sole focus of my heart and mind. This all came about mainly because of a huge "come to Jesus" moment I had last week, and I felt it imperative to put pen to paper and to share with you an explanation of what occurred.

I reached a very deep depression, one that I have never reached before in all of my years. Depression is something that has been a long-term battle for me, but it hit a level that I did not even know it could reach, and for the first time in my life suicide was really something on the table. Being alone was one facet of it, but more than anything it was an echoing refrain from the Enemy, trying to convince me that nothing in my life really mattered anymore. That despite my efforts, it was all going to be in vain. That every breath that entered in my body was somehow a waste of air on this earth. My thoughts scattered and all at once began to free-fall. I felt helpless and alone. Yet then came the thought, am I really doing what God has asked, or am I navigating my own path forward, while only occasionally asking God what to do? Like a ton of bricks, I was hit with the bitter reality that I am either in or I am out with God. I cannot call Him my Savior but treat Him as a phone-a-friend when I end up in a pickle. My life is either His, or it is not. The time of ruling and navigating and forging my own life must come to an end. So, in a way there was a death to self last week, but the godly and correct kind.

Much of what I have fostered for myself in this season was proof of my own immaturity and lack. At that time, I thought I could write my love story but then became disappointed when my actions did not result in what I had hoped. Who am I to blame God for the results when I did not even seek His input in the first place? He needs to be not an afterthought, but the original Giver of thoughts in general. I am coming into reflection of my desperate need for a Savior more than ever.

Humbly, I came before the throne of God in submission, admitting how desperately I need Him. This is not something that will be done only once in my life, but is a daily choice to pick up my cross in humility and follow Him, for it is Him that I desperately need. All at once I had an experience like never before. Like a warm blanket the Holy Spirit came upon me, raining down comfort, peace, and the feeling of being truly known, loved, and accepted even in my brokenness. It is too glorious for the mere words that our language can produce even in its finest and most articulate speech. I am in awe.

And so I place before Him the sacrifice and offering of my time, my will, and my future. It is His glory to author my life, and I genuinely want Him to do so, including my story with you. So, I will let it go into His hands, His timing, and His way. For the first time in my life, I really feel this security unlike ever before. It is not me saying the words in the hope that I can convince my heart, rather it is believing it in full assurance that He is faithful and good, and His plans are for good.

So onward I go, and I know you will be there along the way of this life journey, but for now I am at rest in the inner working that He is doing within me and within you.

All my love,
Your Future Wife

Prayer:

Father God,
Thank You for this man who is reading this letter. Thank You for the time, effort, and intentionality You have had with us both. Break us where we ought to be broken and mold us into the people You destined us to be. Help us as the navigation of it all gets tiring, and help us to remain secure in the good plans You have for us.

In Jesus' name,
Amen

Graduation... Again!

May 2, 2015

Dear Future Husband,

T alk about a milestone week—just, wow! Today I graduated from college. Four years, thousands of papers, and an excruciatingly long final semester, and at long last, your girl is finished with school. Whew! Somehow, despite all the stresses and unexpected aspects of the past four years, I was able to graduate with honors with my degree in English. It is so surreal.

A few months ago, I applied to work for Apple as a creative tech. The premise of the opportunity is that I would go through training to learn some of Apple's specialties, such as GarageBand, iMovie, and the like, and then teach others how to use those programs in the local store. It was a series of five interviews, and I was nearly certain I would be hired, but at the last minute they did not choose me. They said they'd call in six months, which would put us about two months out still, but we shall see. Until then I have decided to take on a job as a nanny, which I have already started.

I've had my nanny job for only a few weeks, but I can already tell I am going to love it. It stirs in me just how much I want kids too. Caring for a four-year-old girl and a two-year-old boy is quite a lot, but there are so many benefits and rewards in the process. From playing dress-up to making cookies, I love seeing their eyes grow in wonder and their faces glow at all the new things they're learning. As adults, we become so used to activities and events that we often forget what it was like to do or see something for the first time. It's a rush and a thrill, and it leads me to wonder if the Lord's meaning behind saying we ought to come to Him with a childlike perspective is just that—we should come with not only a humble trust, but a wonder in seeing things as if for the first time (Matthew 18:3).

For isn't it that way when we receive a Word from the Lord and then see it come to pass? Our hearts may have experienced it before, yet with each time our eyes widen, a grin grows, and the roots of a firmly planted trust expand even further than before. I want to live my life with a child's heart expecting and reveling in what her Father in heaven has in store next. I want to believe His words and truths with a hopeful expectation, without a jaded perspective or fears. The times when I am cynical or suspicious of something, it is not because God has failed me, it is because man has failed me. I don't want to operate with Him as I do the expectations of the world.

All of this brings me to considerations of having kids myself. I pray even now that the Lord builds up in me the skills needed to be a good, kind, and present mom. I want to give them the best that I can give, and I want to raise them well. My instincts tell me that as this nanny job progresses, I will come to know more of what it really means to be a mom. Like a test drive.

Other than that, the summer is set for a lot of travel. First to Minnesota for two weeks to see family and friends, and who knows what might just await me there. After that a trip to New York City for a few days. Life is a beautiful mystery these days, and I for one am appreciating every part both big and small.

What is your summer looking like? Are there dreams and goals and ambitions you have for yourself? What has the Lord planted as a seed in your heart to nourish and grow later on to sprout as a tall and well-established tree? Though I try not to tarry for too long, I think of you often in my daydreams. More than that, I pray for you in my heart. God whispers to my heart more about you as time goes by, and I can say with a fullness of joy that I am most elated to meet you when that day comes. You have a place already reserved in my heart, you know.

All my love,
Your Future Wife

Prayer:

Father God,
Thank You for new beginnings and new lessons learned. Help us both as we navigate, grow, and learn in our own journeys and story lines. I know for now, at least, those story lines are not merged. We are on our own paths that will one day meet, but until then bless this man. Bless him, the work of his heart

and hands, and help him to know Your heart for him more and more each day.

In Jesus' name,
Amen

You're Worth This Wait

September 9, 2015

Dear Future Husband,

I really don't mean to complain, but where in the world are you? I heard an anecdote recently: "Your husband is not lost; he climbed up a tree to get a better look down the path and now he's stuck in the tree." It was meant to be corny, but if you are stuck in a tree, for the love of all that is good, please have someone bring you a ladder and come on down!

There is a battle within as I'm struggling with being content in the present with all that is, and all that I am doing and seeing, but then also longing for the future. Life is a progression, but the steps forward can often move slowly. Much of this is due to the fact that many of my friends are getting married. I'm going on my fifth time being a bridesmaid, and although my heart is beaming with joy celebrating my friends, I find myself waiting by the cake table during the slow dances. In truth it's the wedding I want—it's not the tulle dress or champagne toasts. It's not even the honeymoon. I want the marriage.

I want the marriage with you specifically. I want to wake up every morning next to you, to grow closer to God with you, and I ache to just know you.

I never told you this, but before I started writing these letters, I came to God very vulnerably in a request. I know that many feel more inclined to date around, to get to know different types of fish in the dating pool, but that wasn't my heart. I asked God for His best, and to make it abundantly clear what His best was. In my prayers for you I often ask God for insights and understandings about you in order that I may pray more specifically for you and prepare my heart for yours. I am confident in the whispers and parts about you that He has revealed to me, and I remain confident that despite my aching heart longing to have you now, all that I have patiently waited for will prove worth it.

That all being said, I know that when we come before the Lord and we ask for His best, often it takes longer than we would expect. If we are asking for filet mignon, it is going to take longer to prepare than a TV dinner, but the difference between the two is beyond words. I know that our relationship will be as well, and I am confident in what the Lord Himself is growing in and through me along the way. For example, when I prepare my heart to come before the Lord, I am coming to not only know more about how to ready myself for you, but to see more fully the woman God wants me to be. I feel more driven to explore the Word of God and to richly pray to become a woman of noble character for His kingdom and for you as a wife. It is so much more than just Proverbs 31; it is taking on the posture of women in the Bible who truly were good and honoring daughters of the King.

Lately I've found myself inspired by Ruth. She is one of my favorite gals in all of the Bible. She was a woman who lost her husband and her security and was tasked with making the decision of what to do next. Her mother-in-law, Naomi, told her that she could return to her father's home, which seemed an easy solution, but she kept her commitment to Naomi's family. She honored the commitments she had made to the Lord, and she served Him so well. It inspires me to honor the Lord in such a way today, but there are also aspects that inspire me as I will one day step into the role of being a part of your family. I so sincerely want to bless you and your family, but above all else I want to become a woman of character God is delighted in. My heart is to steward that which He gives me to the utmost of my ability.

And so, though I started this letter aching over being single, longing for the day when I am not alone, I've somehow encouraged my own heart in the waiting and in the continuation of nurturing my own soul, life, and walk as I become the woman God needs me to be as a wife.

All my love,
Your Future Wife

Prayer:

Father God,
I commit my life, my walk, and my innermost self to You and You alone. Father, help me to become the woman You want me to become. Teach me how to be a woman worthy to be called a follower of Christ and help me as I make steps

toward becoming the kind of wife my husband needs. It is my deep and genuine desire to be honorable, loving, and a Ruth-hearted member of my husband's family.

In Jesus' name,
Amen

The Honor of Intercession

June 17, 2016

Dear Future Husband,

It is a strange thing how God can place upon our hearts a push or a nudge toward action in prayer. I consider the countless times in Scripture where someone would be moved by the Spirit of God to intercede, and how the Lord graciously heard such intercessions and acted on behalf of His child. One of the most vivid passages of this was when Hannah the mother of Samuel came before the Lord asking for a son. She did not whisper subtle words, but boldly and passionately wept before God imploring Him to grant her such a petition. That being said, within my own spirit I have felt something richly within to pray for you. So, my ambition for the next thirty days will be to get up at 3 a.m. to pray for you however the Spirit leads me to do so. I am not sharing this as a boasting of my own self; rather, what I hope is that it will later serve as a confirmation to you that during this time our Creator worked in your life. I pray the fruit will become evident, and that it will be clear what He did in your life during this period. You are so prayed for, so desired, and you already occupy my heart and purest prayers.

All my love,
Your Future Wife

Prayer:

Day 1: The Lord led me to pray for your safety. For protection in your daily life and protection from all that may seek to harm you or things that could occur. Safety while driving, while flying, while doing whatever your day might bring.

Day 2: I felt led to pray for your confidence. That your self-esteem may rise and that you will with a humble spirit embrace boldly all that God has designed you to be. That this confidence would differ from pride and arrogance in that your heart would be holy and set apart. That it is evident the Lord abides in you and it is clear that in every action He is your strength.

Day 3: A prayer for your joy. That whatever comes your way in this life, your joy would not be dependent on circumstances but on your relationship with the one who holds your heart, God.

Day 4: Prayers for your work. That the work of your hands and the work of your occupation may be abundantly blessed by God. The things you do and all that you are may receive favor so that the big dreams you have may come to pass.

Day 5: I pray today for your health. Physically that you would be strengthened daily and seek to care for your body well, for it is a temple of the Lord. May sickness not be your portion and may you be given wisdom on how to care for the body in which your spirit dwells.

Day 6: May your spiritual health be blessed beyond measure. I ask God to bless your ears to hear Him more clearly, your eyes to see that which He hopes for you to see vividly, and your spirit to be sensitive to His so that you may know Him better and may follow His lead and direction with certainty.

Day 7: Discernment is a gift of the Lord that we may know Him more certainly, so I pray for your discernment and for wisdom. Lord, please make him a wise man after Your own heart. A man who is willing to submit his will to Yours in order that he may experience what You author in his life.

Day 8: A new heart. Father, I pray Ezekiel 36:26. That his heart may be soft and moldable for what You have for him, that his heart may not be stubborn stone. Father, mold his heart to be like Your heart. Break his heart for what breaks Your heart, and place within him a spirit that desires to follow You and You alone.

Day 9: May he be given an understanding that his life is greatly valuable to You, Lord. May he see that he is part of the body of Christ and serves an important role and function in the church of the Lord. And may these truths drive him toward good ambitions that seek to glorify God above all else.

Day 10: Help him to know his strengths and what to hold on to and what to let go of. Help him build the muscle where he does have strengths that come from You directly and help him to be willing to let go of what is not for him.

Day 11: Build up in him curiosity to dive deeper into the good work You have for him. May his spirit not grow complacent or apathetic in the day to day, but may he have a fervor to go further and higher and deeper into all that You have for him, God.

Day 12: For spiritual gifts. Lord, I am so grateful for the spiritual gifts You have given me so I may know You and the works of Your hands more deeply. Please develop and enhance my husband's gifts that he could know You more deeply than any person he could ever know in this lifetime.

Day 13: Give us a desire for You above all else. Set our hearts, minds, and ambitions that we above all else seek to honor, obey, and serve You in all things. You are our first love, Lord; please let that be the case today and forevermore.

Day 14: May we be equally yoked and suitable counterparts to one another. May we live by Ecclesiastes 4:10, to help each other up when one falls and encourage each other in relationship with God. May the closer we grow in relationship only set us closer to You, God.

Day 15: Create in him a pure heart. One that is not swayed or tempted to act upon sin, but one that takes those things that seek to harm him and brings them straight to You. Help him to rely on You when the Enemy seeks to attack him.

Day 16: Truthfully and boldly I pray for his body to be kept pure. It is a lofty prayer in this day and age when it is so culturally acceptable to sleep around, but Lord I pray this man would not fall into that sin. I pray his body would be kept holy for our marriage. I boldly ask this.

Day 17: Father, I pray his home is protected from the Enemy. We know from Ephesians 6:12 that the battle is not against the flesh, but really is against the powers and principalities in the spiritual realm. Lord, please create a hedge of protection around his home this day to shield him from any work or harmful scheme of the Enemy.

Day 18: Please bless his family. I feel particularly led to pray today for his mother. May our relationship one day be such that we are truly family like Naomi and Ruth, and may she be blessed this day. Thank You God for her and thank You that she raised such a precious man.

Day 19: For his father I pray today, Lord. I pray for his health, his joy, and for his relationship with his son. I pray that he would give him good fatherly wisdom and insights that are like what You give as our Father in heaven. I pray for their relationship to be strong and healthy.

Day 20: Please bless his friendships. Life is hard to go through alone, and we were made for relationship with You and with each other in friendships. Give him honorable and godly men to walk alongside him as brothers.

Day 21: Grant him a circle of people around him who will enrich his life. I pray particularly for a mentor or older friend with great wisdom who can assist him in his walk and life. That someone will come alongside him who serves as a good older brother in Christ.

Day 22: Give him wisdom about those he chooses to spend time with, please. I do not know if he is dating anyone at this time, but if that is the case, the fact that he will marry me is proof he does not marry her. Please help him acquire what he needs to learn in that relationship, but I pray he does not remain in such a relationship for long in order not to create soul ties or cause more harm later on.

Day 23: Teach him now how to be the husband I need. My heart is unique, and I know this, and even how I feel loved and seen is not the same as it might be for another, so I pray now that You will teach him how to love me so that I feel sincerely loved.

Day 24: Teach me how to love him. Please build up in me now what specific ways I can fully help him to feel loved. I want to help this man be all the best that he can be.

Day 25: Help us both to become the people we need to be for each other. Whether that is learned through success or failure, I pray that these vital characteristics would be fostered and grown during this time so that we may be a good and honorable couple.

Day 26: Please give us both wisdom when it comes to financial things. We do not serve or worship money, but money is a part of everyday life and I pray that You would instruct us both in how to handle things when it comes to money and finances.

Day 27: Cultivate in him a childlike spirit. One that is full of wonder and curiosity at how vast and remarkable this world is, one that sees the world wide-eyed.

Day 28: Stir in him a thoughtfulness toward the future, toward what is ahead along the path. Please do this in order that he would not mosey into what is next, but instead be prepared and excited for the chapters to come.

Day 29: Surround him with a truth today that he is wonderfully made and important to this world, to the kingdom, and to his future wife.

Day 30: Abide in him. May Your love, Your light, and Your Spirit abide within this man fully and may every single stitch and fiber of his being know that he matters to You and that You are the Lord of his life.

Lord, I pray each and every single one of these prayers in Your Son's holy name. Lord, graciously hear my heart for this man, and thank You for hearing me as I come before Your throne.

In Jesus' name,
Amen

Planks and Specks

January 4, 2017

Dear Future Husband,

H ow often do we easily find the flaws, missteps, and shortcomings in others but then completely ignore our own personal issues? Or if we do acknowledge them, why do we fail to simply do anything to work on them or heal them? Recently the Lord has been convicting me of the verse in Matthew 7:3–5: "Why do you look at the speck of sawdust in your brother's eye and pay no attention to the plank in your own eye? How can you say to your brother, 'Let me take the speck out of your eye,' when all the time there is a plank in your own eye? You hypocrite, first take the plank out of your own eye, and then you will see clearly to remove the speck from your brother's eye."

I do not want to live a life where I either ignore the planks in my own eye, or acknowledge them but do nothing about them. In sharing that vulnerability and truth, I openly offer my process toward my own self-work. When I started these letters to you, I wanted to invite you into the process of how I became the woman you are now married to. Part of this process requires acknowledging the aspects of myself that need work.

We are much like pieces of wood at the start, each specifically chosen by the Artist to be shaped and formed into a sculpted piece of beauty. The beauty is taken in by others, but the praise goes not to the work of art, but to the sculpting Artist Himself. The wood begins rough and solid, yet within this piece of wood exists the sculpture; it only needs to be revealed in time. For the beauty within to be revealed requires the act of whittling. A knife pierces the wood, again and again, shaving off whatever is not of the sculpture. Scraping and stripping ensues. The wood shrieks out in pain, "This hurts, this hurts!" Yet despite the whining of the wood, despite the resistance of the wood, the Artist knows this must be done for the sculpture to reach its fullest form. It must occur for all the falsehoods and the splintered fragments to be removed. Then at last, even if it seems the process will never end, the Artist dusts off the shavings and what remains is the finished sculpture. Exactly as intended by the master Craftsman. For we are His masterpiece, and it is for His glory that He whittles us into the person He destined us to become. I want to be a willing piece of wood.

Before me lie the habits and struggles I must allow to be shaved off of me. My impatience. My passive-aggressive habits. My self-doubts. My unhealthy coping mechanisms. These rest upon my shoulders like the wood that must be removed for me to be free, truly free, and to truly become myself. Yet I cannot remove them from myself; I need the help of the Artist. So when I ask for them to be removed, who am I to then cry out in pain when He scrapes them away? Why do I fall back into the coping methods I am accustomed to, such as an eating disorder? If I asked for that to be removed, then why do I see if the old chunk that was cut off could fit again?

This process requires placing my will in His able hands. Surrender is required, but after surrender comes obedience and willingness in the marked path ahead. If I truly want to become what I know I was destined to be, I must be willing to be whittled.

Our lives require this type of sanctification. There will be times where you go through it, or I go through it. There will be times when as a couple we share in it and go through it together. My heart for you today is to know that when such times do come, I am here to stand by you. As your wife and your rib. Your counterpart and your safe place. I am yours.

All my love,
Your Future Wife

Prayer:

Father God,
Please mold us, shape us, and carve us to become the people You designed us to be. I know it will hurt and ache, but I also know it will be worth it—not just for the personal reward but so that You will shine and receive every bit of praise for what is presented in us. Create and craft in us Your model and design for Your glory.

In Jesus' name,
Amen

A New Start

September 18, 2017

Dear Future Husband,

I am finding myself back at square one job-wise, it feels like. The past two years I've been working at Apple, and it has been such a learning opportunity full of growth. First Corinthians 1:28 shares how "God has selected [for His purpose] the insignificant (base) things of the world" (AMP). It stood out to me how He uses the unlikely to fulfill His will; rather than calling those who are equipped, He equips the called. The fact that He would pull an introverted, shy, quiet girl to work at such a vivacious, loud, and extroverted store is still astounding to me. Yet He did.

Two years later, He has called me yet again to shift into the next thing that He has for me, this time into teaching. I remember I was prayer journaling when He clearly stated, "It is now time to teach." This caught me off-guard, for I had not considered teaching with my English degree. Sure, it plays right into it, but really? That's the next step for me? I did not fight Him but went forward at His direction.

It was a difficult journey, to say the least, to find the where and how of what to do next. I must have applied to over fifty grade schools, but one day while driving I heard in the back of my head over and over and over again, "Salem, Salem, Salem." I contacted Salem Christian School and was told all the teaching positions had already been filled for the upcoming school year—it was June, after all—but they invited me to interview in case I would be interested in a substitute opportunity. The interview was incredible. The principal looked over my résumé and asked if I knew a Susan Bartnam, to which I happily exclaimed, "Of course! She was my tenth-grade history teacher!" Intrigued, he nodded. The following day I received a call with a job offer: not for a substitute on-call role, rather a full-time job teaching US History, Spanish Elementary, and Computer. I joyfully accepted, but it was what happened next that really blew my mind about what God had in store.

The following day I received a call from Susan Bartnam. She shared how the school had asked her to teach US History again for the next year, but the Lord prompted her not to say yes, but not to say no either. She had wanted to retire, but she felt the need to hold the seat. After my interview, the principal asked her advice because she had mentioned the possibility of retirement. She then knew exactly why she had been holding the seat—it was to save it for me. Mrs. Bartnam had recalled how as a student I had a rare and unique love for history, and how even in high school I had expressed my curiosity about one day becoming a history teacher like her. Rarely do we get the bird's eye view on things, but it was evident that God had placed each and every piece and that this job was for me and me alone. Now I only had three weeks to prepare my lesson plans, but because I had leaned not on my own understanding but followed the winding path He paved for me, I knew I was stepping into a role destined just for me. Wow.

The first few weeks teaching have proven a difficult task—and dealing with these kids is quite the learning curve for me—but I feel right in line with where I ought to be. God is faithful, and He led me according to His plan.

I share all of this to say that when we trust Him, He sees down the road and already has it marked and paved. I cannot say what or when or how things will come at us, the challenges He will hand us, or the hills we will be forced to climb, but I do know we have a big God who goes before us with a steady hand and a well-marked path if we let Him lead.

Testimonies like these add to the trust and faith we can have in Him, and they set a precedent of what He has done and how He can do it again in the future. How kind is our Father to us? How humbling is it that we are included in the things He has for us?

So here I am in this next leg of the journey, and I am excited to see what comes along the way too.

All my love,
Your Future Wife

Prayer:

Father God,
Thank You for well-marked paths, for even when clear answers come in a subtle whisper, You speak to them and You give the insight and understanding we desperately need to do the next right thing. It is for Your glory that these things are accomplished, and it is for even more testimonies of Your great intention in our lives. Remind us of these things when we feel tempted to doubt in the future.

In Jesus' name,
Amen

Lessons Learned

July 8, 2018

Dear Future Husband,

It is incredible how much I have learned in the years of writing these letters. I've learned so much about God and myself, and I've learned how often the courses we mark out for ourselves are not the ones that actually come to pass, but there is a blessing in all of that. I thought the plan I had made with my own pen was correct, but then God intervened.

I made the mistake of thinking that what God had said previously concerning you had perhaps changed, but that one is on me. For God is not a man that He should lie or change His mind (1 Samuel 15:29), and the Word of the Lord stands true, even if what I can see in front of me looks like something different. You see, what I am getting at is that the Lord has given me very specific insights about you, but then along came this other fellow. He did not align with what God had told me about you, but he was *similar, good enough, kind of right*. I think this is where the idea of a counterfeit comes in.

A pastor's wife once told me that often, before that which God has for us comes about, the Enemy will send a counterfeit— something easily accessed that looks appealing but in actuality would be settling. To ensure we are walking in God's best, we must come before the Lord to ask if this is truly what He has for us in His will.

I humbly acknowledge that I nearly fell for the counterfeit of you, but God intervened. Perhaps it is a bad idea to even share all of this, but I feel a peace within knowing that it will be received well and serve as a confirmation to you that God was looking out for us both so that in the end it would be as He saw fit: you and me.

The attempt of a relationship with this other man from the start did not feel correct, but it was a case where I learned a lesson through failing. I am grateful that the Lord let it go only so far before ending things permanently, and this letter certainly will not be a play-by-play of all that we experienced together, but it is part of my story now. I jumped the gun from a place of feeling lonely and longing to be in a relationship, and now the consequence remains of picking up the pieces of my own heart and submitting them back to Christ. What I remain confident of is this: The Lord is good, and He is able to help me going forward even though I have made a mess of things in the past. He is good at helping us clean up such messes.

What is also here in the present is that my hopes were dashed. Grabbing the pen from His hand, thinking that would be a solution to my impatience, only provided a detour that I have the feeling will take me longer now to get back on the correct road. Life can be like a GPS, and if we think we are so sly not waiting in a traffic jam by taking the nearest exit and navigating our own way down roads we may find ourselves lost, running on empty, and further away from the destination than if we had just been patient during the jam. Yet it is not wise to live in the place of regret, nor is it wise to roll over and fester in our shortcomings. Instead, I acknowledge that my own snatching of the quill was out of my own flesh, and I submit that pen back to Him now, trusting His way above all else.

I am certain of this: you are out there. My heart swells in gratitude that He helped me not just dodge a bullet but avoid a future that would not have been authored by Him. He is a good Father and a far better Writer than I, and I trust the story He authors is far superior to any that I could ever ask for or imagine. He said to me recently, "You would have never been satisfied with a basic boy meets girl story." While at first I was a tad offended by such a reply to my prayers, He is right. My heart longs and was made for the grand adventure, not the cookie-cutter Hallmark movie story line. So, I suppose we are at the point in the story where He cleans up the mess I've made in my own flesh, and I follow what He has in store. Of all the stories I've heard, I think your story in all of this navigation is perhaps the one I long to know most. Thankfully I do know the ending to this one, and that is you and I. Forever entwined.

All my love,
Your Future Wife

Prayer:

Father God,

Thank You for divine intervention. Thank You that You let us go only so far before we realize the severity of how desperately we need You as Savior and Shepherd. Thank You for not giving me what I was writing in my own pen, but for retrieving the pen back from me in order to write the story You have authored. Your best, Your way, and in Your book of life.

In Jesus' name,
Amen

A Deeper Relationship

November 9, 2018

Dear Future Husband,

You know the feeling when you're at the pool in the heat of summer? You get a running start and take a deep plunge into the water, and all at once you're entirely immersed. Your head spins a bit, water goes up your nose, and for a few seconds you gasp to regain air, but the adrenaline of that adventure was so irresistible you just want to go again and again. That is exactly how I have felt recently in my relationship with the Lord.

Unlike ever before, I am coming into the depths of really knowing my Savior. Much more than during Sunday services, much more than when listening to podcasts about hope, I have that deep, full, intimate relationship of knowing Him. John 10:14 tells us that He knows us, and the word "know" in Greek is *ginosko*. It means to richly, intimately, completely know someone, as opposed to the other form of "know" in Greek, *oida*, meaning to recognize or recall. I for one want to have a relationship so deep with our Creator that at the end of my life there is that *ginosko* joy that I have reached the end, not just a recognizing like an acquaintance.

Many of these revelations have come by knowing Him more through spiritual gifts. God speaks to His children in many different ways and through the different kinds of relationships He has with each of us. In the same way, I may prefer to text one friend rather than call, and make time for one-on-one conversation with another. I do not love one more than the other, but I meet them where they can be received best and feel the most known by me in the process.

Lately God has been speaking to me most predominantly through dreams, visions, and metaphors in nature. I started having dreams a few years ago, and to be honest it took a long while before I was able to really accept that the Creator of the cosmos would be communicating with little old me through dreams, just as He did with the great men and women of the Bible. Yet He does. These glimpses may come in a dream or in a brief vision in the daylight, but they hold within them a resounding understanding of something that He wishes for me to know. I am ever humbled at each of these little gifts to unwrap and study. They are detailed thoroughly in my dream journals.

Metaphors in nature also seem to have become a primary form of communication. On earth Jesus often spoke in parables to those around Him. These parables would use a metaphor to connect to those in His company, such as a fishing metaphor when He was among fishermen, to get the point across in a richer way than speaking plainly. Being the little nature dweller that I am, trees, animals, and the things of nature seem to be the way to get His heart across to me. Astounded, I sit in awe and wide-eyed wonder at all that He seeks to convey to my heart.

How does He speak to you? In what ways does He unlock and peel back the mysteries of this life, your life, or the world to you? I cannot wait to come to know what stories you have and what places the Lord has led you into. You can believe fully that I will be hanging on every word when you do.

The Lord has been taking me further in the journey than I could have ever expected, and with it, to no surprise, the Enemy has been on me a lot. Spiritual warfare has become a vivid reality along with these new glories to revel in. Yet somehow, despite all that the Enemy has thrown at me, my joy remains. My joy exists in knowing my Savior is at work within me as I am His clay to mold.

Isaiah 45:9 says, "What sorrow awaits those who argue with their Creator. Does a clay pot argue with its maker? Does the clay dispute with the one who shapes it, saying, 'Stop, you're doing it wrong!' Does the pot exclaim, 'How clumsy can you be?'" (NLT). I do not wish to be a lump of clay that argues with its Maker that He is doing a bad job. I am not perfect at this mind you, but still there is that innate desire to just *trust Him.* Why is it that it can prove so hard?

Yet here among all such things are my ponderings and wonderings and all that I am gleaning from this season, and that I graciously leave with you.

All my love,
Your Future Wife

Prayer:

Father, thank You for how You communicate, share, and work within us so that we may know You better and with greater understanding. Father, we submit to You the time, the effort, the hurts, and the joys of this process. You, Lord, are worth it.

In Jesus' name,
Amen

A Marked Place

April 17, 2019

Dear Future Husband,

Recently I had one of the most incredible experiences of my life, and I felt it imperative to share it with you. It was one of those events in life that I believe will prove to be a landmark shift in all that is to come. When Jacob was at Bethel and had the dream of the ladder with all the angels, he had a life-altering encounter with God. God gave him the amazing promise that his descendants would be numerous like the sands of the earth and that God would be with him. Can you even imagine such a dream given from God Himself of what He had in store? Well, I had my own life-altering God story happen this past week.

I was visiting family again in Minnesota and was on spring break from teaching. I spent some time with my cousin deep in prayer. We prayed for many of the people and things going on in the world; we prayed for our own lives, and I spent time praying for you too. I was exhausted and jet-lagged, so we headed back to her house, and I took a nap in her stepson's little toddler-sized bed with Lightning McQueen bedding. The dream began with a view from above of myself sleeping. I could see the green sweatshirt I was wearing, the position I was sleeping in, and the stillness of the nursery. Then a woman entered the room. She was around age thirty with long flowing hair down to her waist. She boldly stepped forward, her stature confident but not at all arrogant. As she gently sat next to me on the bed and lightly placed her hand on my back, I literally felt her hand resting there as an offer of kindness.

Words were not needed in this vision, because it spoke for itself. Whatever this woman had experienced or seen, it was clear she knew exactly who she was and exactly who her God was. She didn't need to even tell me the story; she walked with the kind of confidence one has when they have seen the Creator of the universe act on their behalf. This woman carried the peace of heaven within her. All at once it became very clear to me—she was me! I am her, just not quite yet. I was given the holy and blessed gift to see this future version of me. Not long after, I woke up radically changed.

Since then, I have become captivatingly intrigued by this woman. For she did not worry about the anxieties I carry now, nor did she enter the room with a timid spirit afraid of what the response would be. It was because it was no longer her flesh or her own abilities or strengths that she was leaning upon; she was fully dependent upon her Maker.

It is clear to me now that I am not her, and I dare say when you read this letter, I may not even be her yet. But I will be. And that gives me hope, hope that one day I will be her. So, in the time being instead of becoming obsessed with her, I am going to make an effort to ask God to instruct me, mold me, and change me into that courageous woman of God. For I desire to be such a noble woman.

Proverbs 31, as overused as it can be, offers such an encouraging word for women who are not yet but aspire to be upright and honoring to God. Verses 25–31 really give me the drive to become such a woman as this:

> She is clothed with strength and dignity;
> > she can laugh at the days to come.
> She speaks with wisdom,
> > and faithful instruction is on her tongue.
> She watches over the affairs of her household
> > and does not eat the bread of idleness.
> Her children arise and call her blessed;
> > her husband also, and he praises her:
> "Many women do noble things,
> > but you surpass them all."
> Charm is deceptive, and beauty is fleeting;
> > but a woman who fears the LORD is to be praised.
> Honor her for all that her hands have done,
> > and let her works bring her praise at the city gate.

And so it is my prayer, my honor, my ambition, and my desire to become such a woman as this. Not only for God, but for you too. The idea of being such a woman that I bring you respect is near to my heart too. I want to be that woman for you, my husband, and I want to bring you goodness all the days of your life. However I can add to or bless your life will be my genuine joy.

I felt led to chronicle this surreal vision for you, for the days to come of my life will be drastically impacted because of the gift of sight I was given that afternoon.

All my love,
Your Future Wife

Prayer:

Lord, I come before You humbly and sincerely in a heart of thanksgiving for such a gift to see what You have for me in the future. Please cultivate in me what it means to become this woman and what it means to truly become a wife of noble character. It is my desire to honor You, honor my husband, and fully embrace the path ahead that You have written.

In Jesus' name,
Amen

Dear Future Father

December 15, 2019

Dear Future Father of My Children,

The future has been heavy on my heart lately, specifically the idea that every action we take now comes with a consequence. This consequence could be good, or it could be detrimental, but the choices we make affect such things. This is both a great reason for soaring hope and a warning to beware when it comes to the opportunities we take or dismiss.

As I have come into my third year of teaching, I consider how the choices we make will in turn have a consequence upon our children, be it good or bad. As I am sure you know as you read this letter, it is entirely my heart to be a mother. I want to raise up children who are encouraged and emboldened to love and serve the Lord Himself in every way. Passages in the Bible that highlight how children are not only a reward from the Lord but His heritage and legacy richly indwell my heart (Psalm 127:3). That is not something to take lightly, but to fully consider so that our hearts are aligned with His heart when it comes to raising up His heritage.

It is easy to give a broad statement when it comes to raising children, but what is required more than anything is work in action. One of my favorite action takers when it comes to children is Mr. Rogers. He helped children feel known, seen, and loved, and he completely embodied the gospel in the way he lived his life. I want to take a nod from him with our own children, whether that's doing Bible study with them at night, bedtime prayers, or teaching them to go to God with their problems, questions, joys, and innermost heart. My parents did this with me, and I remember being five years old sitting in my room one night asking God for a little brother or sister. As time would prove, God answered that prayer and sent Gordon. Even as a toddler I was taught that God is real, He is someone we can talk to, and He cares. That was huge for me then and even now as I think back on it.

I also want to instill in our children that we see them, hear them, and desire to know them. It is my firm belief that our children will be people who come into this world to leave a mark for good. We can make a difference for them in how we give them our attention. The more I work with kids, the more it becomes clear to me that in their hearts they want to feel valued, like their opinions and insights matter. Whether it's a show they're really into or art they make, they want to be recognized. Helping their self-esteem will be beneficial I believe in the development of their character. Though I do not know your story now, and in truth I hope you don't share in this experience, my own background was filled with a lot of bullying and hurt. As I was growing up school was not easy, and it was a common occurrence to feel alone, unimportant, and not valuable. We can make that difference in our home for our children—even if the world seeks to counter it—by raising them with a safe place for communication and honesty.

There is no way that we can control the future or the world or culture, but we can raise children with great love. We can plant trees and raise children, two things that can bring something good to this world. I pray your heart is in agreement with mine in that way, and I cannot wait to hear your own heart for our children.

All my love,
Your Future Wife

Prayer:

Father God,
You have planted in my innermost heart and embedded within the fabric of my soul the desire to raise up children, especially children to be raised for Your kingdom. Lord, even now I pray blessings over these future children. Psalm 139 reminds us that even before they come to be on this earth You know them, You have crafted them in Your hands, and they are Your creation. Father, raise me up now to become the mother these children need so that they will honor You above all else.

In Jesus' name,
Amen

The Wife I Want to Be

June 8, 2020

Dear Future Husband,

I doubt this is something guys do in youth group or small groups through church, but for us ladies there always seems to be an evening where we would chronicle our hopes and desires for a husband, on a scribbled list adorned with lots of doodles and hearts over the i's. If you are totally unaware of this practice, then it probably sounds absolutely ridiculous. But the premise was sincere: to list these desires and pray that God would supply a man with qualities that meant something to your heart. Not a list of superficial requests (well, you weren't supposed to) but rather a list of hopes and dreams for such a man that He would send.

I found my list from years ago and to be brutally honest, I was so very naive. None of my requests were sinful or superficial, but they missed a depth that I wish I had during those years. I think many of those shallow puddles of my actions were why the Enemy was able to prey on me as he has in the past few years, but I am grateful that the Lord did not allow me to stay there. It seems that I was flooded by truth, humility, and understanding that could only be learned by experience and God-given wisdom, so that those puddles became deep rivers of desire of what God alone could cultivate.

So below is a revised list, but this time I've included things that I want to become for you. Not to ask God to pluck things from you, rather these are ways in which I want to grow to become the woman you deserve to call a wife and God, a daughter. These are my commitments to you to honor you, uplift you, and be hopefully the woman your heart has been desiring for a long, long time.

1. To the best of my ability, to not lead you into sin. Though the first of my sex (woman) led the first of your kind (man) into sin, I will do my make every effort not to fall prey to the same fate. This will start with a sexual relationship that is honoring and in line with what God says, but it will grow into the other facets of what it means to be a wife who walks in obedience to the Spirit of God so that I may not cause you to stumble or sin.

2. To point you to Christ with God's help. Ecclesiastes 4:9,10 tells us that "two are better than one, because...if either of them falls down, one can help the other up." It is my heart to not only do this, but to also lead you to the cross on a daily basis. I want to be a voice in your life that echoes the lead of the Holy Spirit, and that will always be toward Jesus, not the flesh.

3. To be a good rib. Ribs have many functions. One is to provide a space that allows the lungs to breathe freely while protecting them from injury, and that is my desire in being a wife. I want to be your soft place, your safe space,

where you can breathe freely and openly without fear of harm or attack.

4. To guard your heart. The ribs also serve to protect the heart. The heart is the life source of the body and immensely fragile, so to think that the ribs would be what protects it also sheds light on the importance of ribs themselves. I want to honor, protect, and guard your heart so that it can be safe from harm. It can be soft and function as it should with me surrounding it.

5. To keep you upright. The last thought on ribs is that ribs help keep the body upright. We will rely on each other to keep each other in line and in check, but it is my deeply rooted ambition to help in any and every way I can to keep you upright when possible. This does not negate or take away from the actions and free will you have, but it will serve as my goal to help in every way I possibly can to keep you on the straight and narrow.

6. To let you lead. I will admit there are times when I am a "strong, independent woman" and that fierce boldness overtakes me, but even as much as I find myself being a leader in my job and other facets of life, I know biblically it is right and honoring that you lead. So that God is the head of our home and then you, humbly along with God I will work to let you lead and not question your authority. I will offer insight or learned wisdom when you invite me into it, but in earnest I want to let you take the lead.

7. Capture and remark upon the beauty all around us. It is my suspicion, based on what the Lord has placed on my heart and shared in whispers, that you too are a nature adventurer.

That the beauty of all nature calls upon your heart in such a way that you are vividly and wildly captivated by God's artistry through trees, sunsets, and the like. So, I will capture and remark upon such beauty and share in that wonderment with you.

8. To make a warm nest. In the same vein as before, it is the subtleties of nature that leave me thunderstruck. Today on a walk I came across a bird's nest up in a tree. It was nothing fancy, but in looking at each of the individual leaves, needles, and sticks that it took to make even this little nest, it became clear that homemaking is no small feat. But I am up for that challenge, and my hope is that together we can make our own comfortable dwelling, be it humble or the place of dreams.

9. To encourage you. It's said that there are five languages of love, and it is a total mystery to me what your top languages are, but for me, one I often give is words of affirmation and encouragement. In a way, perhaps that is part of what these letters are: words of encouragement. And so, it is my heart to encourage, uplift, and embolden you so that you feel known, seen, loved, and cherished even on the worst days.

10. To be your best friend. Lastly, it is my vow to be your best friend. A true friend will always be your biggest fan or most truthful critic. A best friend is that and more, and a best friend sticks with you through the thick and thin, the easy and the hard. I vow to be present and to be all you need in a best friend to the highest of my own ability.

It is my deepest prayer before the Lord that each of these may prove true.

All my love,
Your Future Wife

Prayer:

Father, humbly I submit these desires of my heart to You. Father, I know they are lofty and big requests, but I also know that through You and with You all things are indeed possible. Help me to be this woman for the man You have destined me to marry. Help me to be all that he needs in a wife even beyond this list, and, Lord, please help our relationship to be rooted in You and made for Your kingdom.

In Jesus' name,
Amen

A New Year

January 1, 2021

Dear Future Husband,

We both enter into a new year, separately but together in this ever-progressing path of time. As we take the first few steps into this new year, I am intrigued and captivated by all that could await us. My spirit stirs and I wildly hope for the unexpected delights, surprises, and gifts that could be awaiting us as we turn the pages from day to day in this brand-new chapter.

Each year I ask the Lord for a word or phrase to carry with me. Typically, it is a word, but there have been times that He has given me a symbol or idea to wrestle with, to hold, or to expect. This year I was given the words "surprise and suddenly," and I for one am anxiously awaiting all that those big words might hold.

Words hold so much power, and they often shape our perspectives of an event or experience in general. If we go into a situation with the firm belief that ultimately all things may be woven for good, we can more confidently endure the heaviness of the hardships. In the same way, if we assume that the best-case scenarios are evidence of the fruit and goodness of the Lord, we can then set such reminders as Ebenezers (a stone to commemorate God's help) how the Lord was faithful in our lives.

What is your word for this year? What goals have you set for yourself, or what ambitions has God given you to achieve in these next 365 days? Are there things even as you read this letter years in the future that prompt you to ponder what might be just around the corner?

There is the thought too of how God prepares us for what is next. I remember when I was working part-time at a clothing company after teaching school and the Lord placed on my heart to step away from that job for something new. I did not know what the "new" would be, but it was clear that my time working that second job was to come to an end. Before I went in for my last day, I noticed two teenage girls crouched on the ground looking at a little sparrow. The sparrow appeared overheated and needed to catch its breath. The girls were unsure what to do, but I just watched as the little bird let nature have its way. The sparrow took in deep breaths and was still for a moment, and when it was ready it flew off, soaring upward. Metaphorically it was clear to me that the Lord would be taking me into a time when I would be catching my breath before He sent me upward into flight. That proved true in my life as the months would tell, and I often wander back there in my brain at how He represented that so well. What an immense gift of understanding in preparation for what is next.

I consider what things the Lord is growing or preparing in me and in my life as I ready myself for you. For you are in the future, and every day that passes is one day closer to being with you. Perhaps it is my patience being grown, or my willingness to quietly trust that His hand is upon my life even in the unknowns and questions. Or maybe it is just that for today at least I can be as I am and where I am, to be still and ponder and wait and pray and catch my breath before it is time to soar.

All my love,
Your Future Wife

Prayer:

Father God,
Thank You for seasons and for lessons that You graciously give. Prepare us for what is next and for what is now. You hold all of time in Your hands, and it is my prayer that in this very moment there would be a reflection of what glories we have seen and what answered prayers we have in our hands right now. May we be made ready for what is to come and may we in all things praise You, in the good and in the heavy.

In Jesus' name,
Amen

Reflecting Thoughts

June 30, 2021

Dear Future Husband,

H ave you ever stopped to think about the plan you had for yourself and then looked at what your life actually has become? John Piper once tweeted, "Occasionally weep deeply over the life you hoped would be. Grieve the losses. Then wash your face. Trust God. And embrace the life you have." Those words hit like a sucker punch to the gut. You are reminded all at once of the hopes you once had that were dashed, but also the severe reality that you are in and must continue to walk forward into. Memories trickle back of being in high school when they encouraged making a five-year plan and trajectory. Who would have ever thought that life would turn out as it had? Yet somewhere within there is hope.

My plans were all sketched in pencil with bright-eyed optimism. You never sketch out a plan expecting to have holes put in it or doors slammed in your face. You never expect to find yourself wallowing in self-pity, regrets, or uncertainties, but then it must be realized that those feelings are just that: feelings. They are not truths to plant a stake into, and they are not where we are to hang our hats. So where does it leave us after we've allowed these feelings to gush forth from the tears in our eyes and we are left in what is? What I have learned in my years is the solution or cure, or whatever you want to call it, is the surrender of our writing instrument. It's letting God direct, write, and lead our story.

Our culture is so bent on us writing our own tales and endings, but that is in truth an impossible dream. Because there is no way to know what could occur down the line and without fail there is no straight navigation to where we are hoping to end up. The path is marked with rocks and steep climbs and, at times, wrong turns. Yet if we let God be the one leading the path, we can know for certain, with no doubt whatsoever, that He is leading us correctly. That was made very clear and plain to me this past week.

I was in Minnesota on a girl's weekend trip celebrating my friend, Hope, on her thirtieth birthday. We took it upon ourselves to embark on a very courageous endeavor: camping and hiking in the Boundary Waters wilderness bordering Canada near Lake Superior. When we began the hike to our reserved campsite, we were met with thousands of mosquitoes. Thankfully I had an urge to pack DEET in my bag, and I'm glad I did. According to our map, the hike was supposed to be around three miles but it ended up being nearly seven. When we set off, except for the mosquitoes, it was tolerable. Rocks and large steps and a few mud puddles left from the previous day's rain, but overall it was fine. We nearly missed the next part of our route, but thankfully we were only about 100 yards off the trail when we realized we had entered a field and were not on the marked path. Onward we went, peacefully following the marked path ahead. Again, parts were not well defined, but we knew we were headed in the right direction to arrive at the promised campsite. Then came a three-way fork.

To the left, it appeared nothing would be found, and to the right was a mysterious and intriguing feeling in the air. It was hard to say if I felt drawn that way, but there was a curiosity of sorts that I dare say was tempting…which perhaps should have been a clear sign it was not something that was correct. Heading north seemed to be the best, most logical route, but we were deceived into thinking someone had already taken our campsite when we smelled wood burning ahead of us. So impulsively and without checking the map, or even with God, we decided to turn right. We pressed on, walking and navigating toward this potential campsite. When we finally arrived, we were met with more mosquitoes and a bleak musty smell. Though we could feasibly set up camp there, the rushing thought was, "Is this really it? Did I come this far for this?" We had traveled miles down this road to arrive at something that was not worth the distance trekked or the efforts expended. It felt like an utter waste.

Immediately the three of us sprang to action unwilling to accept what was. Instead of sinking into the muck where we stood, we looked to retrace our steps in order to move forward to the correct site. Though this site was unoccupied, it wasn't ours. We had been assigned campsite 7, and even if it took us all day and night, we were going to find campsite 7 and not settle on anything less. I remember asking God to lead us as we ought to go, and He did. We walked miles heading back, landmarks taunting us as reminders of our wrong turn, as we had to journey to that fork in the road yet again. At long last, once the wrong route had been sorted through, we arrived at the fork. This time, we moved forward to the site we were assigned, rather than settling for something else. It took a while and we had lost daylight in our misstep. Our feet ached yet we continued on with flashlights in hand.

Along that journey the Lord whispered to me, "Do you get the metaphor yet?" This simple whisper all at once began to make sense. How we had gotten only slightly off the path in the beginning, but not enough to cause any damage or lose much time. Then at the fork it was clearly evident that we should go straight, but a voice of doubt had caused us to turn elsewhere. The memory of when the Enemy had tempted me to turn elsewhere in the path of dating sprung back in my mind. Thinking of the time I had spent going down that path, the efforts and energy given to that man, I considered how the Lord did not let me settle on that second-best, subpar, disappointment of a landing point. But in order to get back on the right track, I had to go backward to move forward. Time in therapy forced me to go back to the time when I was seeing that other guy, before I could move forward into what God had for me. And all I learned during that period was so vividly represented along this hiking journey. And then when at last I was on the right track again, at the fork, going straight forward was the only way to stay on the path that He had promised and confirmed to me as His best. I humbly asked to know somehow when we would arrive at the point in this hiking metaphor that represented the current situation in my journey to you.

On and on the three of us gals went once again toward our destination, my spirit sensitive to whatever thoughts would emerge or things God would show me. This was a time of metaphor and miracle, and whatever happened next in the journey would prove pertinent in symbolism to the larger scheme of things. We rested on a rock unsure of how long the journey would be. My legs were weary, and my heart whispered, "How much longer?" He whispered, "This is where you are now." Meaning we had arrived at the metaphoric spot of where I am on the journey to finding you. Then a determination came over me as I took the lead of the crew feeling the energy of the Lord upon me, and then right as we turned the corner there was the campsite. I knew at last we were on the right track toward our campsite 7, and I was not far off from the future God had promised. What a beautiful moment of weaving and wonder of two stories, and it was all…*right around the corner.*

And so, by allowing God to lead, to take the pen of my life and author my story, I arrived precisely where my heart desired to be, for it was He who wrote that desire in my heart. I will hold this memory as a secure promise that if in fact I am where He said I am, then you my dear husband are *right around the corner.*

All my love,
Your Future Wife

Prayer:

Father God,
May it indeed be so that he is right around the corner. And may it be so that You use all things, even hikes in Northern Minnesota, to convey Your works and plans.

In Jesus' name,
Amen

A Snowy Day of Thoughts

January 5, 2022

Dear Future Husband,

I am finding myself on a very snowy day here in Richmond, Virginia, which is a rarity of sorts. Especially because two days ago it was 75 degrees and sunny and yesterday was 60 and rainy. Then here on this Monday afternoon the view outside my window is six inches of snow! I must admit that I am eating a large helping of humble pie. I literally laughed at the thought that there would be a chance of snow today, and yet overnight God has flipped it all to a Winter Wonderland. Humbly, I am seeing how like a strike of lightning He can change the entire atmosphere and landscape, all overnight.

Days like this are also good for the soul to recollect and to ponder richly. I am still on Christmas break from teaching, so now is the lull of just being and resting before school starts again. In my own restless spirit, I asked God to make something happen, to move things about, but instead in a gentle whisper

I was given, "You'll thank Me for this rest later; you need it." He, of course, is correct, and it is a time where I can simply rest and consider all that has been happening lately.

Since my last letter there have been some really incredible moments in my walk with the Lord, and I'll share them because they offer a greater view into my spiritual growth. The week before Christmas I came down with a flu-like virus, but its timing was intentional by the Lord. He had me sit the entire weekend to just be with Him. It was like we journeyed through the past three decades of my life and all the refining changes and work that has been done, in particular the past seven years of whittling He's done in me. He shaved away what was not me and left what truly is—the grand design of the Grand Artist.

Where I am finding myself now is in a place of longing, but it is not sinful or full of despair. Instead, it is rather a place where I feel so authentically and genuinely myself that in that rawness, I am eagerly ready to share and be with the one whom God had in mind when He created me: you.

Although I have dated others and admittedly shared far too much emotionally, finding myself in entanglements, God has let me go only so far. Mainly, I didn't have understanding of who I really was to be; it was just more of a general idea. I am so grateful that I had not reached this pared-down, genuine version of myself until now, for it was not given or squandered on anyone else. There is a gift of being in full agreement to become the woman God desires me to be and wholly walking out what that means in attitudes and actions. God told me that weekend that I have gone as far as I can go in personal development on my own; I can journey no further without you. He said that you are reaching that place now...

And so, I am left with this longing desire to wade fully into being with you. I wish to be immersed in life and sharing with you. To offer the fullness of who I truly am, fully exposed and without shame emotionally and physically, to you in marriage. It is a joy beyond words to know that coming into relationship there are no questions of who I am or the facets that combine to make me. What a beautiful gift from the Father to know oneself, and then to become one with you.

He views you as royalty and loves you with a love so profound it astounds me. He offered to me today how He has moved and altered things of my life that I may become who you need—like Esther being prepared for the king. Things like how I dress have changed in order to please Him and to match your heart for a wife. It is my deep desire to be the woman you have dreamed of your whole life, and to be in all things the only suitable woman to fit such a man who honors and regards God as I am confident you do. I have faithfully surrendered things to Him and then had overwhelming joy when He shared that it will be to your liking. Many women may not understand such a heart attitude, but for me it is a gift for God and one day for you as well.

My prayer is that you are coming into such a realization as well, and that somehow our lives will become entwined, in His timing, in His way, and by His will.

All my love,
Your Future Wife

Prayer:

Father God,
I pray for the man You have for me. It is my prayer that You would whittle and remove that which is not truly of him, that which is not Your desire for him. Immerse him in Your Spirit of truth and refinement that in all things he may find himself Yours, truly and wholly and irrevocably Yours and the man that You designed him to be. May he be protected from any snare or scheme of the enemy, and may all things work together for his good and Your ultimate glory. Thank You, my kind and loving Father.

In Jesus' name,
Amen

New Names

April 8, 2022

Dear Future Husband,

It is funny how a single name can immediately invoke a sentiment or opinion with a mere utterance of the lips. These letters, fashioned into syllables, form something more gloriously delicious than the finest creme brûlée, and they work together to fashion *your* name. I daydream and imagine that day I get to write *your* name.

Names hold a lot of significance. They identify who a person is, and for women they can be added to in marriage. Earlier in the year I was given a verse from the Lord to ponder, dwell on, and pray over myself. For me this was an uncommon practice in praying for my own wants. Typically, my prayers are focused on, well, you, dear friends, family, or events of life and the world. Yet here God was imploring me to meditate upon a verse.

It was the night we covered a study of godly light in a Hebrew/Greek Socratic Bible study, and one of my friends offered a verse from Isaiah:

> I will not stop praying for her
>> until her righteousness shines like the dawn,
>> and her salvation blazes like a burning torch. (Isaiah 62:1, NLT)

But God beckoned me further down in the chapter regarding what to really dig into prayer for. He has done this before with verses, but this one was such a shift. It was a call to ask the Lord personally to give me a new name.

> And you will be given a new name
>> by the LORD's own mouth.
> The LORD will hold you in his hand for all to see—
>> a splendid crown in the hand of God. (Isaiah 62:2,3, NLT)

This shook me in a beautiful way. I ruminated upon these verses over and over again. And Isaiah goes deeper in verse 4:

> Never again will you be called "The Forsaken City"
>> or "The Desolate Land."
> Your new name will be "The City of God's Delight." (NLT)

This was a double meaning of stepping into the wondrous light of being God's chosen, God's beloved, and God's bride, but also I could sense the preparation within my spirit that He was calling me into such a season in the natural as well. A season to prepare for what He has ahead.

God often changes the names of individuals before they step into a significant call on their life. Take Peter, for example.

His given name was Simon, but after his time with the Lord as a disciple, he was given the new name of Peter, or "rock." God did this in a radical shift of life as he stepped into his calling.

Or consider Abram and Sarai. After encountering God they were given the names Abraham and Sarah (Genesis 17:5,15). God gave them not only a new name, but a new identity as well.

I dwell on this and the impending promise God gave me that in praying this verse over myself, there would one day be a legal shifting and changing of my own name. You will be giving me part of your name to claim me as your own, and in that you will be a living example of what God did for His bride.

That new name will not be one I take lightly, or something I receive on a whim. Rather it will be something I choose to wear upon my heart with the utmost of gratitude. For it will not be a name I alone chose to take, but a name that was given by the Lord Himself to bestow. One that I will receive as a precious gift, an honor, and a delight.

All my love,
Your Future Wife

Prayer:

Father God,
Thank You for names. Thank You for that which You assign and give us to carry and wear on this earth in the way of names. Let us not become so busy in our own lives that we neglect to recognize the genuine blessing it is to carry, woven within our own names, Your Spirit, Your mark, and Your call upon our lives. Lord, help me to live out the new name You will give in Your timing and all it represents for Your glory and for my husband's benefit.

In Jesus' name,
Amen

Unwrapping the Gift

June 9, 2022

Dear Future Husband,

D o you know one of my favorite things in the world is unwrapping very ornately decorated presents? It is because opening the gift is all part of the experience. There is a sincere joy that erupts as the ribbons and bows are gently pulled back, the tape connecting the pieces of paper is removed, and as piece by piece the true gift within is revealed. The process of getting there is something magical. I have a similar experience to share concerning you—and me to a certain extent—and I wish to offer it to you like the precious gift it has been to my heart.

Though you are not yet in my life, the Lord offered me a gentle but clear warning that our first date will not be as I expect. Truthfully, I do not know just what I expect, but I think at times we can get carried away with setting lofty hopes for ourselves. For someone who resonates deeply with her Myers-Briggs classification of INFP, my imagination is something I attempt to keep leashed so as to not get too carried away with my own heart's wishes.

God impressed upon me that you will be timid to open up, but it was the metaphor He used that really made me realize the gift within that you are, the present that awaits within your heart. He showed me the concept of layers to illustrate what it means for someone to open up. So often when we are protective of what is within our hearts, life has not been kind to us. In an effort to preserve what is left of us, we cover ourselves with armor of a sort. He showed me for you a thick black coat that had protective coating that would keep out the elements. Not a puff coat or one just for the occasional snow day, but one that is made for real snow, real blizzards, real storms that come. This coat allowed for warmth within and protection from all that surrounded.

He told me this layer would remain on initially, but not forever. The second layer was a fleece vest. This vest exposed the arms so they were free to embrace, yet that golden heart within was ever shielded and kept zipped up. Layer three was a long-sleeve, button-up shirt—a flannel, one to keep your tender heart warm and safe. Under that was a simple tee, casual and comfy, signifying the kind of relaxation you'd have in spending a warm afternoon in a hammock with the birds chattering above you.

Then there was a final layer: an undershirt that was steel gray. It was the last remaining barrier, and for good reason too. The impression I got was that this was the level that you'd let a parent into knowing. The kind of undershirt that had the comfort of a pair of PJs. You'd let a mom or dad in at that level, but that was all they'd ever get to see or know. Then at last beneath that was the bare skin—the soft, vulnerable skin that was the door to the heart. It was shared that in marriage I would be granted the access to such a level, one that no one had ever been at before, nor would anyone else ever be. It was for me and me alone to hold and receive such a precious, immeasurably cherished gift, for then a small door would open to your heart. My prayer in writing this is that you know I will honor, respect, love, and revere this gift as the second greatest gift I will ever receive, the first being Christ Himself. For you are that treasure to me.

To love something is to be open to getting hurt, for you are in a place of extreme vulnerability. Yet I sincerely pray you know I understand the gravity of that, and that you can safely open up to me. That is not something I take lightly. This progression the Lord offered me regarding the layers of emotional intimacy is such a representation of the gift that you will be. Metaphors are God's way of conveying something far deeper than we may have gathered otherwise, and, my word, the astounding beauty of this one.

All my love,
Your Future Wife

Prayer:

Father God,
Thank You for metaphors. Thank You for how You can illustrate and explain something in such a way that it radically alters not only our expectation, but our approach in genuinely loving another person. Lord, help me to be a safe place for the man You have waiting for me in the future.

In Jesus' name,
Amen

Worried for Nothing

July 5, 2022

Dear Future Husband,

H ave you ever eaten crow? Because I have. Figuratively speaking of course, not actually eat the bird, because that's gross. But I am in a place to humbly admit that I often eat crow.

Why am I eating crow this time, you ask? Because I am realizing how much time I sincerely wasted over worrying that God would, for some reason or another, fail to keep His word to me.

By nature, I have a tendency to doubt, worry, or fret. The story of Peter walking on the water and falling has resonated deeply with me. I know he fell because he took his eyes off of the Lord, and that was how we ought not to live, but as someone who is often waiting for the other shoe to drop, I can relate. Yet recently I am coming into deeper truths than ever before, one of which is that in the story of *Cinderella* the second shoe never actually dropped. She was able to place it on her foot and prove that she was indeed the one the prince had been searching for. Other truths are that God is faithful to every single word. Every last one.

He spoke to me about trusting Him with a situation a few months ago. It looked entirely impossible and hopeless, and I could not in my own limited understanding see how there was any way possible that He could bring what He promised to pass, and yet He did.

It is often that we find ourselves in a place completely unsure of how He could possibly change a situation. Consider Jesus' words in the story of Lazarus:

> Now a man named Lazarus was sick…So the sisters sent word to Jesus, "Lord, the one you love is sick."
> When he heard this, Jesus said, "This sickness will not end in death. No, it is for God's glory so that God's Son may be glorified through it." (John 11:1–4)

The words here are very intentional and important to understand. Jesus stated that the sickness would not *end* in death, and furthermore that the Son of God would be glorified through the story. When Jesus arrives to greet the sisters of Lazarus, they explain that their brother had died four days prior. In that moment it would be assumed that the word of the Lord had proven false, for Lazarus was literally rotting away in the grave—but it wasn't the end of the story. Jesus promised that it would not *end* in the death of Lazarus, and it did not.

Here is how the story ends:

> Then Jesus looked up and said, "Father, I thank you that you have heard me. I knew that you always hear me, but I said this for the benefit of the people standing here, that they may believe that you sent me."

When he had said this, Jesus called in a loud voice, "Lazarus, come out!" The dead man came out, his hands and feet wrapped with strips of linen, and a cloth around his face. Jesus said to them, "Take off the grave clothes and let him go." (John 11:41–44)

In this the word of the Lord has proved true. When we are in places where the situation looks completely hopeless, we need to remember *this isn't the end.* God has the final say. Always.

So I marvel in pure reverie at the fulfillment of what God offered to me in so many areas. I stand in an awestruck posture of peace and thanksgiving that the Lord proves true.

Let us hold firmly to that in the days when we are tempted to doubt whether He will keep every last word.

All my love,
Your Future Wife

Prayer:

Father God,

Thank You for Your faithfulness. Thank You that You are not a man that You should lie nor change Your mind (Numbers 23:19). Rather, You are faithful to every word. Lord, help us not to be like waves tossed about in doubt, but rather help us where our faith is lacking. Help our unbelief so that we may stand firmly upon the Word of the Lord in all times.

In Jesus' name,
Amen

Letting You Lead

July 22, 2022

Dear Future Husband,

You may notice that I can be a little stubborn at times… and fiercely independent. You'll probably chuckle at that sentence, but for the record I am well aware of that myself. What is arising in me is the concept of letting you lead.

Ephesians 5:23 states, "For the husband is the head of the wife as Christ is the head of the church, his body, of which he is the Savior." This verse strikes me because it is something that requires adjustment on my end. Not in Christ leading me, as a part of His body, but in preparing for the new season that awaits me of allowing someone else to lead me in addition. I heard a pastor once say that if I don't agree with something in the Bible, it isn't the Bible that needs to change, it's me. In coming before God, I need to see where and how my thoughts or attitudes need adjusting in order that I may truly abide in the abundance of what is correct. In my side I find a thorn that is poking me that these verses are somehow incorrect, and that I ought not to let you steer the ship. But that thorn is not of me, and it isn't something I want to carry into our future marriage either. So, I wince, and I ask the Father to help pluck it out of me that I may be free and clear of anything that does not belong.

It is a beautiful thing to let you take the role of guiding us as well, for I trust you will be a good leader. I am no longer limited to just the scope of what I myself can offer, but I am invited even further into the grounds that you have covered. I see our marriage metaphorically as if the two fields that we both own will merge, and we are invited into each other's fields to explore, wander, and tend. There is so much ground to cover and so much to joyously inhabit with it all.

There have been examples of when the woman did the leading, and I saw how off-kilter the relationship became. I was witness to a marriage where the woman called all the shots. She dictated how they would get engaged, how things would operate at home, and even how he was to get a job. I saw this once bright man reduced to a doormat before my eyes, and it saddened me. Marriage is a partnership, but there is a reason why husbands are to be the head of the home. I say this with a vulnerable and humble offering that it is my heart to trust and respect where you guide us. I know that you will do a good job of this because of your personal relationship with the Lord. I trust that what you hear from God is tested and true and that your heart and intentions are pure. I believe you will be a wise man after God's own heart. Truly, if it is God leading, then ultimately there is no worry or fear, because things will be in correct alignment as they should.

I offer this up not to pressure you, but out of respect. I believe you are an honorable man who makes wise and methodical decisions with discernment given to you from God. I will be here when you desire to know my opinions on things, and I will always be rooting for you, but you don't need me to boss you around. I will not mother you; I am sure you already have a wonderful mother, and you don't need two. I will stand as a partner to you while letting you sail the ship. It is evident you are letting God guide you in that navigation.

I trust you.

All my love,
Your Future Wife

Prayer:

Father God,
Thank You for how You guide us, instruct us, and give us the correct formula for how families should align. I think of 1 Corinthians 11:3: "But I want you to realize that the head of every man is Christ, and the head of the woman is man, and the head of Christ is God." Lord, it is my desire to follow that which You have instituted with great esteem and obedience. Please give my husband a hunger and desire for You and help me as a wife to pray for him and be the partner he needs. Lord, guide us that we may follow You correctly.

In Jesus' name,
Amen

Love Languages

July 30, 2022

Dear Future Husband,

I want to speak and understand *your* language, the language of your *heart*. My goal and desire is not just to *know* the language of your heart, but to fully and completely *live out* what it means to understand the language of…you. This requires actually living out your love language.

These letters I am writing are ones in which I am partnering with God in preparation for joyously and graciously becoming your wife. I get to pray for you specifically and attune my heart to hear what God has to say about you as an individual before you are even with me. You are a man who receives and gives love in his own specific way, and the honor I will one day have to offer love to you and accept love from you will be remarkable. It is something that deserves to be richly prayed about so that I love God's son (you) in the correct way.

Yet, our love language is not the sole way we communicate as humans, for each of us is wired in a unique way in which we live our lives, respond to situations, and operate on a daily basis. The Myers-Briggs test is one that has proven a fantastic aid to me in my relationships with family and friends, and I find it useful in understanding my own self as well. I fall into the INFP category on that test. I cannot wait to know what you are on that test as well.

It will serve as a great resource to me in understanding the inner workings of both you and I so I can grasp the reason behind our responses. It also is helpful so that grace can be given where it is needed, and deeper discussion can be opened to better understand each other.

Perhaps this is a good time to offer my own "secret codes" as well—the pieces that comprise me and the minute details that I seldom offer about what really makes me feel loved, seen, and known. So, here goes.

Taking notice of the small details about me helps me feel seen. My dad has done a good job of this, and it always touches my heart when he does so. I love Reese's Pieces and it seems whenever we are on a trip and stop at a gas station, he somehow remembers that I love that candy. It always ends up in the bag to go, even if I am snoozing in the passenger seat. It's a 99-cent item that just helps me feel known and seen.

It means a lot to me as well to have authentic words spoken. I am not one for attention and I don't like being put on the spot in front of others, but it means a lot when a sincere word is given to me. Most of my life I have hidden in the background trying to appear invisible, but I think even the most ghostlike of individuals who share this sentiment appreciate when they are acknowledged for more than just their existence.

All of this is to say that my desire is that we love one another in such a way that we both feel completely known, seen, and understood despite our flaws, shortcomings, and insecurities. I take the nod from Adam and Eve in that they were naked yet unashamed in Eden. It is my heart to accept you as you are, scars and all, and help you to feel safe and desired even with them.

All my love,
Your Future Wife

Prayer:

Father God,
Thank You for the gift of love, and the truth that we all love in different fashions. We are uniquely crafted individuals who give and receive love in distinct ways that are never the same twice. Lord, make us aware of how to make each other feel loved, and give us the ambition to softly and tenderly love each other as we ought to. Help us to imitate You in love, for You are love, God.

In Jesus' name,
Amen

Parents

August 2, 2022

Dear Future Husband,

For years, I asked the Lord for a relationship with my future in-laws much like that of Naomi and Ruth. These two women were committed to each other by a deeper bond than legalities (as Ruth was Naomi's daughter-in-law); they were connected to one another through the love of God. I wanted the kind of love, respect, devotion, and kinship that was evidently rooted and cultivated by God. I sincerely hope that will be the case with your parents—that I will cherish them and thank God for them, and that the feeling will be mutual.

My heart is that we seek to honor both sets of our parents in the ways that we can. I want your parents to feel that they are gaining a daughter just as I know my parents will feel that they are gaining a son. Whether we live close to both sets of parents or not, I sincerely hope we will help them all to feel valued, important, and loved. Furthermore, all the blessings that can be fostered in embracing what family really and truly is as God designed in the Word.

So, I was thinking perhaps, if it would be fitting with your heart's desire, we could set a weeknight every week or every other week to have the parents over for dinner. I so admire how the Jewish people in the Old Testament would seek to have family dinners weekly, sharing richly in one another's lives. I don't want it to be one where we are holiday-only children but where we are involved in doing life with one another.

If we do not live nearby, I was thinking weekly FaceTime calls could be sweet, as well as making it a point for visits, either in our home or theirs.

Honoring parents is not just a biblical encouragement and one of the commandments, but it is something that is a gift to us too. We can learn so much from our parents, be it from their mistakes or successes, their best recipes, or their life advice. Sometimes it may be the things we wish not to pass down, but we can relearn together what is best and most beneficial for our own little family.

I think we have a very wonderful opportunity to integrate our families as well. Growing up, at holidays we would go to my dad's family or to my mom's, but there never seemed to be the idea that we could have them both to our home. It may be a lofty aspiration, but I love the idea of merging our families so that our kids are not so defining of "mom's family" or "dad's family" but rather just "my family." So, although it might be a lot of work, I was thinking we could consider hosting one of the holidays at our home. I want them all to feel special and loved.

Just some thoughts.

All my love,
Your Future Wife

Prayer:

Father God,
Thank You for the blessing of families and thank You for the specific parents You chose for each of us. Lord, although they can frustrate us at times and although they all have their shortcomings (as do we), they are still our parents, and we want to honor them. Please give us the wisdom and guidance on how we can honor our parents and offer an environment for our kids where they feel the support and love of their grandparents. And, Lord, thank You for my future husband's parents. It will be a great joy to learn from them and see what remarkable people raised such a remarkable man.

In Jesus' name,
Amen

My Banner is Clear

September 7, 2022

Dear Future Husband,

D id you know I am your fan? Seriously, I am. I don't even
know you beyond that which God has revealed to me
about your character, and I am already such a fan of you.

I sit in a position of wide-eyed wonder at how the Lord
describes you when I pray for you, and how He refers to you
with such love and unfettered joy. It is a profound view that
I have to see the inside story of you, even as I await coming
to know you, and I think perhaps an eternity of thanking
God may not be enough time to properly praise Him for you,
my dear.

It is through the lens of Christ and in abiding in Him
that we are given this sharper glimpse of reality. Instead of
making judgments from the outside, instead of concluding
our opinions of things based off assumptions, we are granted
the access to clearly grasp what is, not merely what it looks
like. It is through Christ that I have been offered the sincere

honor of truly seeing you as the Father sees you and the reality of who you are as a man.

It is through an intimate relationship with the Lord that I have come into a deeper understanding of seeing others as He does. The prophet Isaiah gives us insight about Christ:

> The Spirit of the LORD will rest on him—
> > the Spirit of wisdom and of understanding,
> > the Spirit of counsel and of might,
> > the Spirit of the knowledge and fear of the LORD—
> and he will delight in the fear of the LORD.
>
> He will not judge by what he sees with his eyes,
> > or decide by what he hears with his ears;
> but with righteousness he will judge the needy,
> > with justice he will give decisions for the poor of the earth. (Isaiah 11:2–4)

In the same way, when we are abiding in Christ and Christ in us, we too have the same viewpoint to see not with natural eyes but with spiritual eyes of truth. Paul says it in another way in 1 Corinthians 2:

> We do, however, speak a message of wisdom among the mature, but not the wisdom of this age or of the rulers of this age, who are coming to nothing. No, we declare God's wisdom, a mystery that has been hidden and that God destined for our glory before time began. None of the rulers of this age understood it, for if they had, they would not have crucified the Lord of glory. However, as it is written:
>
> > "What no eye has seen,
> > > what no ear has heard,

and what no human mind has conceived"—
the things God has prepared for those who love him—

these are the things God has revealed to us by his Spirit.

The Spirit searches all things, even the deep things of God. For who knows a person's thoughts except their own spirit within them? In the same way no one knows the thoughts of God except the Spirit of God. What we have received is not the spirit of the world, but the Spirit who is from God, so that we may understand what God has freely given us. This is what we speak, not in words taught us by human wisdom but in words taught by the Spirit, explaining spiritual realities with Spirit-taught words. The person without the Spirit does not accept the things that come from the Spirit of God but considers them foolishness and cannot understand them because they are discerned only through the Spirit. The person with the Spirit makes judgments about all things, but such a person is not subject to merely human judgments, for,

"Who has known the mind of the Lord
so as to instruct him?"

But we have the mind of Christ. (1 Corinthians 2:6–16)

These verses are ones that I have pondered and prayed about, and they encourage me to boldly allow Christ to reveal truth to me through His lens, and it is through that understanding and lens that I will see you. I grasp the way the Lord delights in you. The Lord sincerely and truly adores you. You are His son, and the man you choose to be is someone God rejoices in, as do I.

I am here to stand on this earth as your biggest fan along with Christ, to cheer you on in the victories, in the places where you succeed. And the places where you fall short, I am here to lift you up, to pray for and with you, and to encourage you in the choice to try again.

When your favorite sports team loses a game, you don't throw in the towel. You cheer at the points that are scored, and you hope for another shot in the future.

My banner is clear that I am for you, and I will stand by you in all the seasons. I believe in the man God has made you to be, and I am thankful to be the woman who is called to be your biggest fan. At times your strongest critic, but always there to celebrate the victories, big and small. I'm waiting here with joy and expectation cheering you on, and I always will be cheering you on. Win or lose, you can count on that.

All my love,
Your Future Wife

Prayer:

Father God,

Thank You for this man You have for me. Thank You for the true honor to see him in a way no other soul ever will—the intimate and intricate behind-the-scenes view. Lord, I'm grateful that, through Your Spirit, You have enabled me to profoundly comprehend some of what You have purposed and intended for this man. Help me to be the biggest fan he needs, help me to support him in his efforts, and most of all help him to live out the path You have destined for him. Help guide my heart with clear and vivid discernment and clarity so that I may be well prepared as his wife.

In Jesus' name,
Amen

Specific Prayers

October 14, 2022

Dear Future Husband,

Currently I can only pray for you in a broad sense—a kind of aerial-view prayer because of unknown details where your identity is shrouded in mystery. I long to stand before you and know the intricate details of your days, to have the particulars of what life looks like for you unveiled. Then I will rejoice to lift you up before our Father in heaven with intentional specifics in prayer.

Even now, it is a great delight to me that I can offer up before the Lord particular requests, praises, and desires on your behalf. I desire to love you both wholly and holy. I desire to love you wholly for the man you are, idiosyncrasies and all. I also desire to love you in a holy sense, that is, in the true definition of the word—to be set apart. A wife loves her husband in such a way that their love is set apart, unlike any other love in her life. That is why prayer is so necessary and imperative, and why even before really knowing you I want to be a woman and a wife who prays for her husband in a holy manner.

Though there are days when my curiosities about you beset me, I am certain you will be far beyond all that I could ask for or imagine. The burden within me to not merely pray for your heart to know and love the Lord, but to intercede for you in distinct ways is something I count as a glorious gift, a calling bestowed on your future wife.

All that being said, I beseech the Lord to hear my innermost heart laid out before Him at the throne.

All my love,
Your Future Wife

Prayer:

Father God,
In humble, awestruck wonder I stand silent before You. For it has been Your hand leading, guiding, pruning, and orchestrating every intricate aspect of this story. The stories You write are wild and so magnificent that even our heightened imaginations could scarcely compare. With a heartfelt gratitude I step in to pray for this man who is one day to be my husband.

Lord, I pray for his heart, that he would increasingly hunger and yearn for You. That he would wander into the depths of the glories that You have for him to explore and know Your character, as if he were an explorer entering into the vast unknown with courage, intrigue, and curiosity about what lies ahead. May the song of his heart be one that sings of Your grandeur and truth and reflects Your heart.

May the desires that are planted within his heart be ones that You have planted, and ones that we come together to cultivate with Your leading, so that the fruit that we both bear may be to Your glory.

Weave within him an assurance of who he is in Your eyes and assist me in how I may help to make this man feel truly secure. Father, I delight in the hope of him. I delight in him because in him I vividly see You at work in this story. I recall the vision I had of this man some time ago as Your apprentice in a carpenter shop, and that is what I pray he will exactly be. A man who crafts beauties in the way that he has been instructed and learned from his Father. It is ever captivating to see a son imitate You in his approaches to life. I pray my future husband will take such an approach. From how he loves to how he handles adversities; he is in every way a man in Your own image.

Attune my heart to hear the whispers You convey and the nudges You give so that I may serve You well above all else, and in doing so serve him well as a wife and one day as a mother to his children. Embolden me to hone in on the specifics that are for me to investigate with Your shepherding.

Father God, thank You for my future husband. You alone deserve and shall have my praise for all of eternity, but with it I cannot even fathom how to begin to additionally thank You for this man. With heartfelt humility, I am honored to be the helpmate of Your beloved son one day.

In Jesus' name,
Amen

Healthy Arguments

October 18, 2022

Dear Future Husband,

I am ever learning and growing in this life, and something that has really astounded me in the past few months is how God can help us to unlearn things as well. From childhood we are wired and programmed in a certain fashion. The habits we develop, how we approach and operate in situations come from the training we receive as children. We are taught from a young age how to act in various situations. We watch what our parents and those around us are doing and mimic their behavior, but that does not always mean it is right or the best way.

My parents are wonderful people who sincerely love the Lord, but they are also flawed human beings, just like me. As a child I watched how they handled disagreements and arguments, and in time I developed my own ways to respond when things get heated. Yet, God has been training me how to handle confrontation in a way different than I had developed.

Conflict is not my favorite thing in the world; in fact, I have been told by my bosses that I am "conflict avoidant." I freeze up and try to avoid issues to the utmost of my ability, and at times it does not bode well for me. When there is no way out of the "battle royale," I do what I grew up seeing. I stand stoically like my father, my voice heightens like my mother, and I cry.

I have been placed in a journey of relearning what I have known for so long. This retraining came about through an issue with a friend. She was frustrated while planning her wedding and took out her frustration on me. One could say I am an easy target as a punching bag, but that did not make it correct. She harshly attacked me in text, and my blood boiled. She asked if we could speak in person, to which I acquiesced. Before she came over, I prayed asking God for wisdom, while also seeing if He could get me out of the confrontation. It was then that He brought *you* up even though you were yet to arrive in my life. He said, "How you handle tonight will be indicative of how you handle confrontation in your marriage." I audibly let out a frustrated sigh. But God had a lesson to show me.

Instead of coming at her with all of my defensives and listing all the things she had done to wound me over the past several months, I did as the Lord prompted, second by second. He told me to not speak but to listen and allow her to let out her anger. As she did, it became evident that she was upset at the situation, not at me. Then and only then did God allow me to speak the truths He had revealed to me, and I did so in a calm and respectful tone. We actually ended the evening in a hug and not a single cross word or hurtful sling was spewed from my lips.

As I processed this with God later, He explained that what I had learned growing up, and what I have seen in conflict management around me, was incorrect. I am not to take my issues to the other person until I have taken them to God first, and not every issue needs addressing with the other person. I can take my hurts, my sadness, my wounds to the Lord. He wants me to, and after doing so then I can take what He has shown me to the other person. He also highlighted to me the importance in marriage of listening, really listening, so that you feel heard. I want to be your safe place, where you can speak and be vulnerable and express what is going on, knowing that someone who cares hears you. You are not just speaking to the wall; I am actively listening.

We are not against each other either, because at the end of the day we are for each other. I am on your team, and at times we won't agree on something, but at no point do I quit being on your side. It is God and us versus the issue, and my heart is that we confront situations with this in mind, taking issues to God together and forging ahead with His leading in every situation. We need to take into account all the other factors and issues we are both battling, whether it is opposition from the Enemy, work stress, lack of sleep, or even hormonal issues at times.

I am for you, and I want you that to know I am always on your side. Just because I have been taught one fashion of handling conflict, that doesn't make it correct, and so I desire to continue in the retraining God is doing within me so that I may be the wife you need.

All my love,
Your Future Wife

Prayer:

Father God,
Help us both as we deal with confrontations and arguments.
Lord, calm our hearts before You as we confer with You first;
lead us to handle a problem in a way that honors each other
and most of all honors You.

In Jesus' name,
Amen

Entwined

November 9, 2022

Dear Future Husband,

Of all the letters I have written to you, there is yet to be one in which I convey how I am increasingly grateful for the fullness of what it will truly mean to be husband and wife. How I cherish the truth that, when God sees fit to bring you forward into my life and I into your life, I will be able to be a wife to you, in every facet of the word.

As I was growing up, sex was portrayed in so many different ways. For some it was spoken about in such a way that it was perverse, dirty, something to be ashamed of to even utter. In other spheres it was talked about in such a way that it was so cheapened, of so little value that it sincerely saddened me. For me it has always been something of such high value, such a set-apart and truly holy meaning, that I hate even calling it "sex," for it is so much more than just a physical act.

The way in which it is spoken about most frequently in a first time is that one would "lose their virginity," but that isn't the case here. It is not my set of car keys that I have lost. I am losing nothing; rather I am giving something that I have saved with the greatest respect and tender protection for you and only you. On our wedding night it is something that I can offer to you in sincere love, something that I have chosen to honor our Lord with in saving such an act for the one He asked me to save it for. To me there is no loss, only gain for us both.

When I was younger it was not that I was without natural desires, but there did not seem to be much temptation. I wasn't some lustful being consumed with this carnal hunger within. Waiting is not as much of an issue when love isn't at play, but the more I grow and learn what love really is in the godly sense of the word, the more I long for that Song of Solomon kind of love. I did a lengthy study on Song of Solomon, and what I concluded in the end was how deeply I desire such a holy and pure love between the two of us. A love that is truly the connection of souls in our rawest, most vulnerable form. One that is rooted in Christ, one that is of His will, and one that is only for us.

I also realized that any previous relationships I have been in were really more of an entanglement of emotion. There are two men I could more or less say I was in "love" with, but as I view it in retrospect it was really more of a fleshly love tied up in entangled knots rather than a true godly love in which souls began to entwine. What I desire for us is an entwining of souls, spirits, and hearts.

And so, even after our long-awaited wedding day has passed, the purity of our relationship shall remain. For we will be pure and correct in standing before God because we have waited as He has asked. We don't lose purity in marriage; we continue it together as one.

All my love,
Your Future Wife

Prayer:

Father God,

Thank You for the gift of marriage and for the gift of love. Thank You that a man and a woman can come together in marriage to become one holy couple. Lord, as we grow closer to the day of our future marriage, there is a good chance there will be the temptation to enjoy what is holy ahead of time, but Lord we delightfully seek to honor You in this way. As difficult as it is, Lord, I ask that You would give us the strength to not cave into temptation, rather to wait so that we can—without shame, guilt, or frustration—enjoy the gift of being truly one as husband and wife.

In Jesus' name,
Amen

It's Not Supposed to Look Like Anyone Else

November 20, 2022

Dear Future Husband,

The Lord once told me that our love story will "never look like anyone else's because it's not supposed to." That phrase held weight not only in expectation, but in the freedom of allowing God to hold the pen of our story. In a world where we are told to write our own destiny, the idea of allowing God to have the pen is a very uncommon concept.

Living authentically intentional in all ways is something rare in the world. It is often replicated with contrived branding by the world. There seem to be plastic counterfeits produced daily with a label marketed to make one think something is authentic, when really it is not. Yet the actual living out of such a mission of genuine authenticity looks quite different. Within this there is a deep, deliberate journey taking place. From the outsider's perspective it just looks like a long time to wait for a mystery man, or perhaps to some, it could look overly religious and nutty. Yet, at the core, what it really is within is an intimate experience with God to ensure that His will, His desires, and His direction were clear and unmistaken. For that, every second will prove worthy and sacred.

From my side of things, what this looks like is understanding all that God had revealed to me about who you are and your role in my future life. It is not taking a hunch, hope, or hint of anything and running with it straight to the altar; rather, it is holding gently in my hand this offering of God and bringing it to His throne. It looks like allowing years of refinement under fire to take place while pondering the Word of God and allowing His Holy Spirit to encourage me when my own spirit was weak. It looks like surrendering what I thought dating should look like and exchanging it for what God Himself has written just for us ahead.

I cannot wait to hear your side of the story. What you have known and seen, and all that God has been doing within you. What lessons you have learned, what you have overcome, and how God directed and guided you along the way. My guess is that it is beyond anything I could even imagine.

This love story is not a typical boy-meets-girl scenario by any stretch of the imagination. He has made that very clear. But instead it is a carefully crafted story that the Lord Himself is writing. He knows our two hearts could handle such a story and that we could be trusted with it, because we did not rest in our own sufficiency but abided fully and completely in trusting Him and His timing ahead.

To whom much is given much is required, but what a gift that He has supplied all we needed for every step to reach the destination that awaits us both.

Somehow within I know you will be worth the wait, trust, and winding-road journey it will take to get there. Yet beyond anything else, the greatest revelation is that the greatest love of all is the love of God Himself. For so long I thought I needed a spouse to make me whole, when really God as our first love is the greatest gift of all. When we love Him first and most, every other love becomes all the more enriched and enchanting. Because I love Him most I can love you in the best way possible.

All my love,
Your Future Wife

Prayer:

Father God,
To You and You alone is the glory of the story of my future husband and me. Lord, it is a story written by Your hand before time even began, and yet to see it unfold will be nothing short of glorious. Glorious to live in, but glory in every form to Your name alone. Father, I know I have had my tearful nights of depression, doubt, and desperation, but I am grateful that I can say You never left my side. Furthermore, You know what is best for precise timing that I am not given what I want before I am ready for it. I believe in Your best in Your best timing.

This experience has been unlike any other, and it was always meant to be like that. Thank You for guiding us both, directing us both, and leading us both on a path that will lead to exactly where we need to be.

In Jesus' name,
Amen

The Rib that Fits

November 29, 2022

Dear Future Husband,

Have you ever seen the play *Les Misérables*? A young woman named Cosette has just met the man she will one day marry. She is aglow with the enchantment of literally love at first sight, but as she is processing, she has an overwhelming realization of what her life has been thus far. In the song, "A Heart Full of Love," she asks, "What's the matter with you, Cosette? Have you been too much on your own?" That line is something I have identified with for years—the feeling of being on my own for so long that even the idea of merging a life is a foreign concept to me. Yet I am met with the curiosity of an enormously wonderful new life where I am not alone anymore, and what a beautiful truth that is to ponder.

There are times when the Lord will drop a word of knowledge to me, or a command to me to walk out in obedience. Sometimes it is an invitation to pray for another person, or send them a text just to check in. Without fail it always proves important that I walk forward even when my own heart may not know what the path will look like. Recently I heard the Father very firmly say, "You will fit into his life, not the other way around." Knowing this was not something of my own imagination or heart, I soberly held this word in my hand to follow correctly in what that genuinely means.

The more I pray into that word, the more I come into the beautiful truth that I am not always going to be on my own, and the choices I make have an impact not only on myself but on both of us. Like how a rib fits into someone's side, so I will fit myself into your life.

This does not throw my own hopes and ambitions away, but I have a responsibility to you to honor and respect you in consideration of my own actions. Currently my choices are to honor God first and foremost, and that will not change, but what will change one day is that the things I do will honor God first and then you. For it is correct that I do so as your wife.

Genesis 2:18 says of the first wife ever how she was made to fit for her Adam: "Then the Lord God said, 'It is not good that the man should be alone; I will make him a helper *fit* for him" (ESV). My desire is to fit however God would see as correct for you, my Adam.

This concept is pretty counter to the narrative of society. We live in a world of self-centered individuals where it is all about "me, me, me" but there is something severely lacking in that. Because marriage isn't about me, and it's not even about you, it's about God and about us as one.

And so, I write all of this to say I want to shift from being on my own for these thirty years that I may correctly fit into what God is calling me into. When I have outgrown my current season and life, I will fit into the new life with you. I am excited to fit into that very soon.

God is my first love, and He has my commitment and obedience first and foremost. I know that we will have hopes and desires about the things we want, but when we delight ourselves in God and follow His direction, and drink in the delight of walking together in His path for us, I believe therein lies a deep well of abundance for us both.

All my love,
Your Future Wife

Prayer:

Father God,
Help me to be the wife I am called to be. I want to vibrantly live out Ephesians 5:22–24: "Wives, submit yourselves to your own husbands as you do to the Lord. For the husband is the head of the wife as Christ is the head of the church, his body, of which he is the Savior. Now as the church submits to Christ, so also wives should submit to their husbands in everything." Lord, give me the wisdom and tools and guidance I need that I may do this to not just honor this man You have for me, but ultimately honor You above all else.

In Jesus' name,
Amen

Don't Look Back

December 27, 2022

Dear Future Husband,

I have been thinking a lot about the past and what it means to let go of what we leave behind. During my time in the Word I came across Isaiah 43:18–20:

> "Forget the former things; do not dwell on the past. See, I am doing a new thing! Now it springs up; do you not perceive it? I am making a way in the wilderness and streams in the wasteland. The wild animals honor me, the jackals and the owls, because I provide water in the wilderness and streams in the wasteland, to give drink to my people, my chosen."

I began to think about how there are so many beautiful things that await us, but in order to fully experience them we must leave the past behind. Not in every case, but many times the past serves as chains upon us. We drag those chains into the present if we do not let them go. What if instead of continuing to hold on to those chains we allowed God to release us from them and to heal us of the marks they have left upon us? What if we stopped looking back and we kept moving forward?

There is also the aspect of what it means to look forward and not back in order to really enter into God's best. In Genesis 19 there is the story of Lot's wife. Lot, his wife, and daughters were told to leave Sodom and to not look back. Lot's wife made the choice to look back and because of this she had the consequence of turning into a pillar of salt. Although we may not turn into pillars of salt, there are consequences for when we look back at something that we were told to leave behind.

I write this all to say that whatever either of us may have in the past that we have been told, or know, we should let go of, let's do so in obedience. I don't want to spend the rest of my life looking back when I know there is such a better future ahead for us both. There is also the thought of letting go of the things we regret. We have all fallen short of glory, and we have all made mistakes. Just because we have made mistakes in the past does not mean that we should not forgive ourselves. If God has forgiven us, then we should forgive ourselves. If we don't, we are somehow saying that we know better than God, and that is incorrect. So, I pray that you will forgive yourself as He has forgiven you. Be free!

I want you to know as well that I accept you where you are and what your past holds. God knows truly that there are aspects and parts of my story that I regret. There are places where I stepped outside of God's will and ran after my own selfish ambitions or drove straight into the ditch of fear in decisions, but those mistakes are not the defining marker of who I am. I am who God says I am, a forgiven and beloved daughter of the King. In the same way, whatever baggage or mistakes you carry, I want you to not fear sharing them with me. I am here, one sinner to another, ready to accept and love you and to together try again tomorrow as we follow after Christ. God has brought us both so far. I know for me at least He has done a great and intricate work within me and I am no longer a slave to the past. So let us embrace and fully enter into freedom. I'm here waiting for you on the other side.

Let's not let a hiccup ruin a song that has been sung for a long time.

All My Love,
Your Future Wife

Prayer:

Father God,
We know that You are a good Father with good plans ahead for us both. Father, help us not to become convinced by the Enemy that what is behind is somehow better than what is ahead, and also help us to embrace the light of hope that rests within us that there is so much good to be seen this side of heaven.

In Jesus' name,
Amen

My First Love

January 1, 2023

Dear Future Husband,

It is a wild thing to me that I have been writing these letters for so many years. When I began this journey I must admit there was not just a curiosity of who you would prove to be—the man behind the mystery—but there was also perhaps this idolization of marriage as well. An idol is not just some carved golden calf, like the one the Israelites worshiped in the desert while Moses was on Mount Sinai. It is anything that comes between God and us. I must vulnerably admit that I have at times let the idea of marriage or the hope of marriage become an idol in my life. I forgot my first love of God.

Thankfully God did not allow me to remain in that place. There is a huge difference between conviction and condemnation. Condemnation is rooted in shame, and that is not from God, as it says in Romans 8:1: "Therefore, there is now no condemnation for those who are in Christ Jesus." Conviction, on the other hand, is when God brings to our attention areas where we are not living in alignment with His Spirit, will, and desire for our lives. He kindly convicted me of the realization that in many places in the past I have allowed the hope of marriage to really become an idol. Not that I would worship you, but that I would place you before God in my attentions and affections. I am so grateful that it is on this side of marriage that He brought that to my attention, so that I can change now and be aware in the future that it is something the Enemy might try again. Because when all the fog clears my head and heart, my genuine desire is to love our God first and foremost above all else. It is only then that I can properly love not only you, but anyone else.

As I consider who I was when I began writing these letters, I see the change in myself over time. I am so very grateful for the patience He has had with me in taking the time over all these years to grow me into a better woman. As a young woman it was so easy to set my own plans and hope God would bless them, when in fact they were so fleeting and shallow. Instead, it is a much more wonderful way to live to allow God to write the plans of life, and to see Him bring to pass things so far beyond all we could ask for or imagine. Proverbs 3:5,6 has been richly on my heart recently with this sentiment: "Trust in the LORD with all your heart and lean not on your own understanding; in all your ways submit to him, and he will make your paths straight." Even when we don't understand "why" things are the way they are, it is because we have a limited understanding. He sees everything, and He is worthy of our trust in the timing, the approach, and the path of every aspect of our lives.

So, I write this to say that I will love you, but never more than I love our God. I am grateful to say that, and I believe you will say the same to me one day too. For if we love our God first and foremost only then can we properly love one another.

All my love,
Your Future Wife

Prayer:

Father God,
Thank You for conviction. Thank You for being my first, my best, and my truest love. Thank You for the relationship You have grown between us and thank You for never leaving my side. Help me to always keep You first and foremost and help my future husband to do the same, that we may walk in the abundance of what it is to love as You would desire us to.

In Jesus' name,
Amen

My Prince Will Come

January 3, 2023

Dear Future Husband,

I believe you will come. I really, really do. I just passed my thirtieth birthday a few months ago, a point where most people begin to lose hope. But I am somehow struck with a deepened hope within my spirit.

This hope is not one I can claim of my own, because in my flesh I am quick to fret and worry, yet I am overcome with a deep peace that I know can come only from God. I have a sense of knowing that He is worthy of my trust even as I await the fulfillment of the seed of promise He has planted within my heart.

Second Timothy 2:11–13 shares,

This is a trustworthy saying, for:

> If we have died with him, we will also live with him;
> if we endure, we will also reign with him;

if we deny him, he will also deny us;
if we are faithless, he remains faithful—

for he cannot deny himself. (ESV)

He is faithful and worthy of our trust, even when it seems hopeless. He is also faithful, even when we are faithless.

I wish I could say that I have been perfect on this journey, that I haven't fallen into pits of despair and wallowed in downward spirals wasting time waiting for this man God has promised me. But then I take a step back and realize what a limited understanding we really have of the world. Isaiah 55:8–11 gives us a firm reminder:

"For my thoughts are not your thoughts,
    neither are your ways my ways,"
        declares the LORD.
"As the heavens are higher than the earth,
    so are my ways higher than your ways
    and my thoughts than your thoughts.
As the rain and the snow
    come down from heaven,
and do not return to it
    without watering the earth
and making it bud and flourish,
    so that it yields seed for the sower and bread for
    the eater,
so is my word that goes out from my mouth:
    It will not return to me empty,
but will accomplish what I desire
    and achieve the purpose for which I sent it."

He knows much better than we do, and His ways are far higher than our own. In the same way, if God speaks something, it must come to pass. I think about creation week when He said, "Let there be light," and atoms began to move and obey so that there was indeed light. So, if not only light came forth because He spoke it into being, but He spoke the entire universe into existence, then why am I limiting Him now? Instead, I am choosing to stand firm since the day He spoke to me that I would be married; I trust that things began to change and shift in the natural world so it will prove inevitable that you will come into my life and I into yours. He is not asking me to do the "how" but rather to walk in obedience in the meantime.

So, yes, one day my prince (you) will come. Until that day I will continue to pray for you, I will continue to lift you up to the Lord, and I will do as He asks, knowing deeply within that He wastes nothing. He does not waste a day, a moment, or a breath of our own.

All my love,
Your Future Wife

Prayer:

Father God,

Thank You for all of Your precious promises in Your Word. Thank You that I do not have to have it all figured out, I just need to obey and to trust in You. You are a good Father and You give good gifts. You are worthy of my trust, and You are worthy of my time during the wait. I know it will prove worthwhile.

In Jesus' name,
Amen

Dear God

Dear God,

I want to truly thank You for the person who has come along on this journey in reading this book. It is evident that there is a curiosity, an earnest desire, or a nudge upon the heart of this person for the potential of a future spouse. That is where we come before You.

More than likely it is within Your will and plans to bring this person to a kingdom spouse— someone who will truly seek to honor You, our Lord, and Your kingdom here on earth while doing life alongside this person in a true partnership.

Meeting, talking, dating, and all the parts in between can appear daunting and intimidating—always wondering if you are marrying the correct person or what the future holds. Lord, I pray that the person reading this right now would surrender all of these questions, concerns, and fears to You. You are a good Father who seeks to give good gifts. Jeremiah 33:3 assures us that You are kind in that if we seek Your heart You will reveal the hidden and secret things. So, Lord, we ask for peace, revelation, and Christ-focused understanding in relationships and dating. Lord, we pray that every false voice, every thwarting spirit, and every opposing Enemy would be silenced in the name of Christ Jesus. We pray that Your voice of truth would reign supreme and be the only voice heard. And, Lord, we pray that fruit would be evident in this couple, and that the fruit would be that of love—true and pure, godly and holy.

Embrace this person and wrap Yourself around her, Lord. Provide for her in ways her heart aches to be known, seen, and loved. And, Lord, set this person on a path that she may truly and wholly become the person she is destined to be in You and for her spouse.

In Jesus' name,
Amen

Hey, You

Dear Reader,

Hello again. At this point it almost feels as if we are kindred spirits, friends, for along the pages and scribbles of these letters a journey has been taken together. A journey that from the outsider's perspective has appeared short and simple, but within the details is shown to have been far more intricate and loftier than originally expected.

You have your own journey that you have been trudging into as well. It is not something where you are at a starting point, for much of the path has already been covered. Rather, you are continuously moving toward the open road that is ahead of you—perhaps now with ideas or perspectives to ponder or take to the Lord for your own story.

God is the greatest storyteller of all. He authors stories beyond even our wildest dreams, and time and time again it proves that He is not limited or predictable. Ruminate upon that richly—He is not limited to what you think might happen, or what might make sense in our human logic. He is so far beyond even our most calculated or educated of guesses. Yet, the stories He writes are ones that are the best of all for these reasons.

And so, get excited about the story He is writing for you. It is an adventure tailored and crafted for you and you alone. No story is ever duplicated; it is a custom fit that is made solely for you—the torn pages, the ink splotches, and the happily-ever-afters included.

The purpose of this book is not to commission you to start writing your own letters to your future husband, although that is a beautiful gift you could offer him. Rather, what I encourage you to do is to reflect upon the beauty of your own God-written story and stand in awe at how much the Father cares for you and for the man you will one day marry. Your story matters, and it is one only you can live out.

And so, if you feel so inclined, pick up a pen to recall all that has been, and all that you are becoming, but let God have the instrument to detail out all that is to be in your life. For He is authoring a story so lovely, so enchanted, and so exceptional that it could only ever fit you.

All my love,
Cally

P.S.

One more thing…

More than likely you are curious about how these letters will be given, and I'd like to offer a behind-the-scenes look at how they will be unsealed.

Within a Red Wing shoebox, a stack of letters has grown over the course of nearly twelve tedious years. One by one, these notes written on scraps of paper or torn-out journal pages were placed within brown envelopes with a small wren stamped on the front. Currently these letters are at around three hundred in all. I tied them together in batches of fifty, wrapped in a Cinderella blue ribbon.

On the morning of my wedding I plan to place this cherished box, containing the journey of a young girl into a woman ready to take on the title of wife, into an old suitcase. Along with the box of letters will be a few heartfelt gifts and a long letter explaining the contents. The suitcase will be "the only baggage I will bring into our marriage," as a humorous piece of symbolism, however audacious that sentiment may be.

I plan to attempt to keep these letters a surprise to him, which will be exceedingly difficult as this book may arrive before he does, but there is a sense of mystery and intrigue in it all as well, just as this entire journey has been. In fact, I will share how this book ever came to be. To paint the scene, it was early in the morning on a blustery Monday in November when I was brewing coffee and the Lord whispered to me, "What would you think about writing a book about the letters you've been writing to your husband?" To which I offered a steady "maybe." The following day I received an email from my publisher. My first book, *Hang in There, Girl,* mentioned that I had been writing letters to my future husband for over a decade, and the publisher thought it would make an interesting book. I knew it was confirmation of the heart of the Lord. It was also indicative to me that very soon He would be sending my husband, and I am confident in that promise even as I continue to wait. After years and years, at long last the one God had placed on my heart to wait for will arrive. I think that is what faith really looks like, waiting with expectation.

Reading through my letters over the years was a nostalgic treasure to myself to recall the girl I was at eighteen. My wide-eyed hopes and ambitions would rise and fall, but in the course of time my faith would deepen and grow as well. I went from making plans for myself and asking God to bless them, to instead standing with palms open and heart surrendered to whatever He would call me to. The greatest gift of these years is not the destination of a wedding altar; it was coming to know my Creator in a richly intimate way. Receiving a husband will only add to the richness of that relationship with God, for through the lens and heart of God I love the man He created. I will love him better and more accurately because of the alignment of relationship I have with God, and I will see him as he truly is, as he is in Christ.

And so, I await with hope and expectation because our God is not a God to disappoint, and He is faithful to the end of the age.

All my love,
Cally

Acknowledgments

To the Lord Jesus Christ, I give you all glory, honor, and praise, for without You none of this would be possible. You have all my gratitude from this side of heaven to the next.

To Julia Baldini, my sister, my ally, and my best friend: Thank you for your endless encouragement, kindness, and having my back on this earth. This book would not exist without your pep talks and prayer calls. I never knew what it was like to have a friend who sticks closer than a brother until I met you, and I love you so dearly.

To Victoria Martinez, my sweet friend who believes with childlike wonder in the God-written fairytales life can have, thank you. Your support and your genuine spirit remind me that happily-ever-afters can come true.

And to Jenae Stinchcomb, thank you for being such a vessel of the Holy Spirit and for being you. I am so deeply grateful for the friendship we share and it is a joy and honor to do life with you.

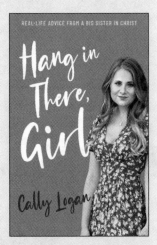

BEAUTY FROM ASHES
Donna Sparks

In a transparent and powerful manner, author Donna Sparks reveals how the Lord took her from the ashes of a life devastated by failed relationships and destructive behavior to bring her into a beautiful and powerful relationship with Him. This inspiring story will encourage you to allow the Lord to do the same for you.

Donna Sparks is an Assemblies of God evangelist who travels widely to speak at women's conferences and retreats. She lives in Tennessee.

www.donnasparks.com

www.facebook.com/
donnasparksministries/

www.facebook.com/
AuthorDonnaSparks/

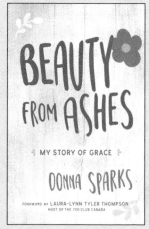

ISBN: 978-1-61036-252-8